Table of Contents
Spelling Homework Booklet
Grade 4

Proud Prince of "Vowel-Aire"

The short vowels **a, e, i, o** and **u** have disappeared into the air! Add vowels to make words from the following letters. Write each word on the line.

1. k __ tch __ n _____
2. v __ g __ table _____
3. h __ sp __ tal _____
4. r __ ct __ ngle _____
5. sk __ l __ t __ n _____
6. j __ n __ tor _____
7. b __ bsl __ d _____
8. cl __ s __ t _____
9. ut __ ns __ l _____
10. __ ctop __ s _____
11. cuc __ mber _____
12. sh __ mr __ ck _____
13. s __ dd __ n _____
14. f __ n __ sh _____
15. p __ pp __ t _____
16. c __ nt __ loupe _____
17. f __ nt __ sy _____
18. b __ tht __ b _____
19. pr __ nc __ p __ l _____
20. ch __ ck __ n _____

The prince has changed the station on his boom box. Now the consonants have disappeared. Fill in the blanks with words from page 2, and then write each word on the line.

1. o __ __ o __ u __   _____

2. __ a __ __ __ u __   _____

3. __ o __ __ i __ a __   _____

4. __ e __ __ a __ __ __ e   _____

5. u __ e __ __ i __   _____

6. __ a __ __ a __ y   _____

7. __ __ e __ e __ o __   _____

8. __ a __ i __ o __   _____

9. __ u __ __ e __   _____

10. __ u __ __ e __   _____

11. __ __ i __ __ i __ a __   _____

12. __ a __ __ a __ o u __ e   _____

13. __ __ i __ __ e __   _____

14. __ u __ u __ __ e __   _____

15. __ o __ __ __ e __   _____

16. __ __ o __ e __   _____

17. __ __ a __ __ o __ __   _____

18. __ i __ i __ __   _____

19. __ e __ e __ a __ __ e   _____

20. __ i __ __ __ e __   _____

Computers to the Rescue!

Enter the words on the computer screen into the correct data bank by writing them on the lines.

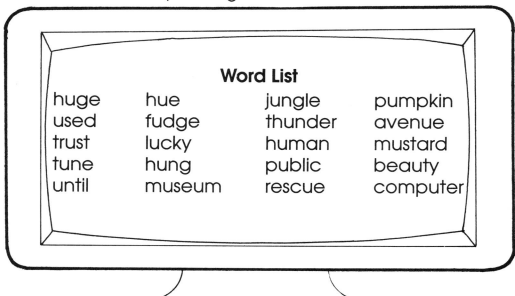

Word List

huge	hue	jungle	pumpkin
used	fudge	thunder	avenue
trust	lucky	human	mustard
tune	hung	public	beauty
until	museum	rescue	computer

y͞oo **Data Bank**   ŭ **Data Bank**

_____   _____

_____   _____

_____   _____

_____   _____

_____   _____

_____   _____

_____   _____

_____   _____

_____   _____

_____   _____

Circle the misspelled words in each sentence. Write the words correctly on the lines. **Challenge:** Try it without looking at the previous page.

1. I like musterd on my hotdog. _____

2. There is a hudge dog that lives on Grant Avenu.

   _____   _____

3. The show was on publik television. _____

4. Rescu 911 is on TV on Tuesday night. _____

5. Tim loves punkin pie and peanut butter fuge.

   _____   _____

6. You can always tust a good friend. _____

7. The muzeum was painted a brownish hew.

   _____   _____

8. Lightning and thundder came with the storm in the jungel. _____   _____

9. That hunam being's beuty is more than skin-deep.

   _____   _____

10. The seatbelt hunng out of our yused car.

    _____   _____

11. We can play a tun on our cumputor.

    _____   _____

12. We are luky because we can stay up untill 10:30.

    _____   _____

Aviator Hotel

"Fly" these **ā** and **ō** words from the Aviator Hotel to the correct landing strip by writing them in alphabetical order. Fasten your seat belts!

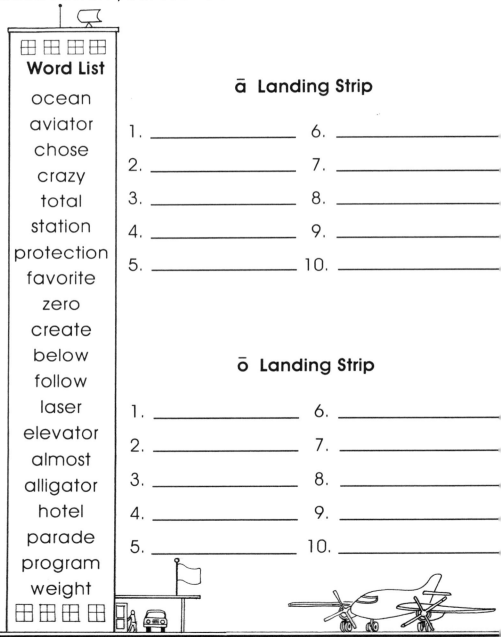

Word List

ocean
aviator
chose
crazy
total
station
protection
favorite
zero
create
below
follow
laser
elevator
almost
alligator
hotel
parade
program
weight

ā Landing Strip

1. _____   6. _____
2. _____   7. _____
3. _____   8. _____
4. _____   9. _____
5. _____   10. _____

ō Landing Strip

1. _____   6. _____
2. _____   7. _____
3. _____   8. _____
4. _____   9. _____
5. _____   10. _____

Here is your flight plan, Spelling Aviator! Write the correct word by each clue. Earn your wings if you can do it correctly without using the Word List on page 6.

1. a beam of light _____

2. safety _____

3. not quite _____

4. first choice _____

5. for overnights _____

6. less than one _____

7. a show _____

8. opposite of above _____

9. a bus, train, radio or TV . . . _____

10. floats, bands _____

11. 94 pounds _____

12. the sea _____

13. picked _____

14. all of something _____

15. a flyer _____

16. zany _____

17. a reptile _____

18. to invent _____

19. tag along behind _____

20. "Going Up!" _____

The Secret Pirate

Ahoy, Matey! Fill in the missing letters of these $\bar{e}$ and $\bar{i}$ words. Write the boxed letters on the lines below to find the name of a famous pirate.

Word List

ceiling
supply
either
motorcycle
female
pirate
meteor
deny
chief
surprise
idea
reply
secret
lying
peanuts
behind
greeting
awhile
bicycle
believe

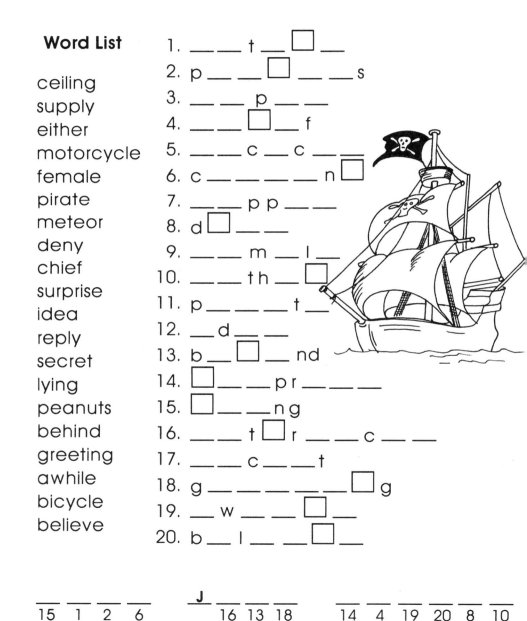

1. __ __ t __ ☐ __
2. p __ __ ☐ __ __ s
3. __ __ p __ __ __
4. __ __ ☐ __ f
5. __ __ c __ c __ __
6. c __ __ __ __ n ☐
7. __ __ p p __ __
8. d ☐ __ __ __
9. __ __ m __ l __
10. __ __ t h __ ☐
11. p __ __ __ t __
12. __ d __ __ __
13. b __ ☐ __ nd
14. ☐ __ __ p r __ __ __ __
15. ☐ __ __ n g
16. __ __ t ☐ r __ __ c __ __
17. __ __ c __ __ t
18. g __ __ __ __ __ ☐ g
19. __ w __ __ ☐ __
20. b __ l __ __ ☐ __

__ __ __ __   J   __ __ __   __ __ __ __ __ __
15 1 2 6   16 13 18   14 4 19 20 8 10

Use the Word List to complete this wordsearch. The words will be across, down or backwards. The ship's gold is yours if you can also find the "secret pirate's" name!

s	t	v	r	l	a	w	h	i	l	e	g	b	x	f	y	n	g
c	e	d	f	o	c	r	l	v	g	w	l	f	h	m	n	w	r
g	r	e	p	l	y	w	f	p	b	d	r	e	w	f	e	s	v
y	c	h	v	l	c	g	r	o	e	t	e	m	v	c	d	h	x
f	e	s	h	x	w	k	a	n	l	f	p	a	g	v	n	g	c
h	s	h	w	c	h	i	e	f	z	c	h	l	v	h	b	d	l
p	d	o	z	w	c	v	b	m	r	d	z	e	w	z	h	x	a
w	e	i	t	h	e	r	x	c	l	b	n	c	h	r	t	v	r
h	c	m	x	s	c	v	k	e	x	p	l	r	z	e	n	p	v
b	l	h	s	u	r	p	r	i	s	e	y	b	l	v	c	i	x
e	y	f	n	p	g	b	l	l	f	a	j	i	h	l	d	r	p
l	m	t	y	p	u	k	c	i	d	n	m	c	j	i	e	a	n
i	c	w	e	l	x	z	b	n	g	u	e	y	b	s	x	t	e
e	r	p	d	y	v	t	s	g	x	t	s	c	v	n	l	e	v
v	g	f	l	b	d	v	d	r	c	s	y	l	m	h	o	i	c
e	k	l	b	e	h	i	n	d	h	z	n	e	c	o	f	a	d
o	z	c	w	n	d	f	x	s	n	b	p	f	s	j	w	l	y
w	y	d	f	r	b	r	w	t	u	a	v	c	e	g	g	w	p
k	m	o	t	o	r	c	y	c	l	e	h	y	g	n	i	y	l
h	t	m	n	g	r	b	o	n	m	d	n	k	l	o	v	p	h
l	g	c	j	h	v	s	h	p	x	i	c	o	f	l	n	m	r
f	m	g	n	i	t	e	e	r	g	h	l	r	s	x	k	s	l
l	g	o	p	v	c	r	c	v	g	r	b	v	p	f	g	h	o

A Royal Appointment

Hear Ye! Hear Ye! You have an appointment with the king to unscramble these royal words. Write them on the lines, with a regal flourish, of course!

1. covie   _____
2. pintemaptno   _____
3. soyin   _____
4. talyyol   _____
5. lofi   _____
6. ommelpnety   _____
7. ijando   _____
8. davio   _____
9. mytenjone   _____
10. lorib   _____
11. noij   _____
12. potsadinip   _____
13. polis   _____
14. yolar   _____
15. foyluj   _____
16. yanno   _____
17. stomi   _____
18. tinjo   _____
19. liibong   _____
20. cohcie   _____

Royal Word List

appointment	spoil	loyalty	boiling
employment	broil	annoy	adjoin
disappoint	foil	royal	avoid
enjoyment	join	moist	joyful
choice	joint	voice	noisy

Proclaim the royal syllables! Find and write the words to fulfill your royal spelling duties.

oy – 2 syllables

_____

_____

_____

oy – 3 syllables

_____

_____

_____

oi – 1 syllable

_____

_____

_____

_____

_____

_____

oi – 2 syllables

_____

_____

_____

_____

oi – 3 syllables

_____

_____

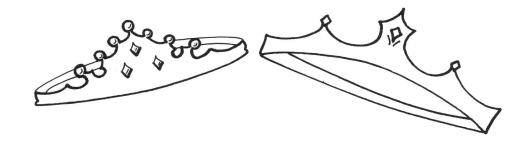

The Sparkler Party

A	B	C	D	E	F	G	H	I	J	K	L	M
21	22	23	24	25	26	1	2	3	4	5	6	7
N	O	P	Q	R	S	T	U	V	W	X	Y	Z
8	9	10	11	12	13	14	15	16	17	18	19	20

Use the code to write these /är/ words. Finding all 20 words earns you an invitation to the "Sparkler Party!"

1. 22 – 21 – 12 – 1 – 25 _____

2. 1 – 21 – 12 – 24 – 25 – 8 _____

3. 13 – 10 – 21 – 12 – 5 – 6 – 25 – 12 _____

4. 23 – 21 – 12 – 1 – 9 _____

5. 13 – 14 – 21 – 12 – 14 _____

6. 21 – 12 – 7 – 19 _____

7. 2 – 21 – 12 – 7 – 6 – 25 – 13 – 13 _____

8. 23 – 21 – 12 – 8 – 3 – 16 – 21 – 6 _____

9. 1 – 21 – 12 – 22 – 21 – 1 – 25 _____

10. 19 – 21 – 12 – 24 _____

11. 23 – 21 – 12 – 24 – 22 – 9 – 21 – 12 – 24 _____

12. 2 – 21 – 12 – 24 – 6 – 19 _____

13. 22 – 21 – 12 – 22 – 25 – 12 _____

14. 10 – 21 – 12 – 14 – 19 _____

15. 13 – 23 – 21 – 12 – 26 _____

16. 13 – 2 – 21 – 12 – 5 _____

17. 24 – 21 – 12 – 5 – 8 – 25 – 13 – 13 _____

18. 23 – 21 – 12 – 10 – 25 – 14 _____

19. 2 – 21 – 12 – 8 – 25 – 13 – 13 _____

20. 7 – 21 – 12 – 22 – 6 – 25 – 13 _____

/är/

Join the party! Use words from page 12 to fill in the blanks.

1. We grew onions and corn in our _____ .
2. Mom's _____ matched her blouse.
3. They watched _____ racing at the fair.
4. The _____ and Air Force fought in the desert.
5. We brought kittens home in a _____ box.
6. I could _____ believe my eyes!
7. The _____ carried coal down the river.
8. A _____ is similar to a fair.
9. It was hard to see in the _____ of the cave.
10. She had a _____ for her eleventh birthday.
11. My mom plants many flowers in our _____ .
12. A _____ warning was posted at the beach.
13. Gentlemen, _____ your engines!
14. Bob bought a Fourth of July _____ .
15. Do you recycle your _____?
16. Most spiders are _____ to humans.
17. The ship's _____ was headed for Canada.
18. The family room had a brand-new_____ .
19. My dad and I go to the same _____ for haircuts.
20. Do you know how to shoot_____?

How many did you get correct? _____

(17 – 20) You're a sparkler!   (7– 11) You fizzled out!
(12 – 16) A real fireball!   (0 – 6)   A dud! Try again!

©1992 Instructional Fair, Inc.   13   IF0146 Spelling

The Perfect Shirt

Write the **er, ir** and **ur** words on the correct T-shirt. Trace over the letters **er** in purple, **ir** in red and **ur** in yellow. Design and color sleeves to create a perfect shirt!

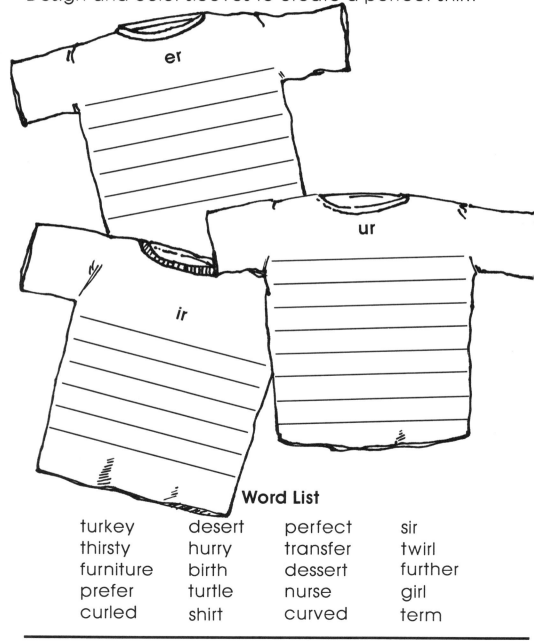

Word List

turkey	desert	perfect	sir
thirsty	hurry	transfer	twirl
furniture	birth	dessert	further
prefer	turtle	nurse	girl
curled	shirt	curved	term

Use the clues to complete the puzzle.

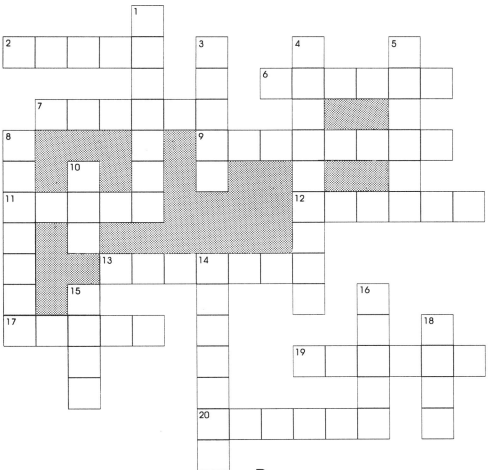

Across

2. medical helper
6. not straight
7. would rather have
9. exchange
11. item of clothing
12. hard-shelled animal
13. beyond
17. spin around
19. rolled into a ball
20. Thanksgiving fowl

Down

1. ideal
3. act of being born
4. tables, chairs, sofas
5. sandy area
8. cake, pie, cookie
10. term of respect
14. needing to drink
15. female
16. rush
18. period of time

Review

Pages 2-3   Circle the ĕ and ĭ vowels.

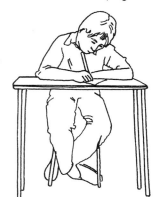

rectangle   kitchen
principal   chicken
skeleton   utensil

Pages 4-5   Fill in the correct word.

rescue

beauty

computer

1. That horse is a _____ .

2. The printer on our _____ doesn't work.

3. John will _____ the kitten.

Look up and write four more ū words. Use these in sentences on another paper.

Pages 6-7   Fill in the boxes with the correct letters. Write these words in alphabetical order.

favorite

create

ocean

_____

_____

_____

Pages 8-9   Make word pyramids for these words on another sheet of paper.

believe

surprise

chief

Example: deny

d
de
den
deny

©1992 Instructional Fair, Inc.   16   IF0146 Spelling

Pages 10-11 Write the words. Then circle each prefix and underline each suffix.

disappoint   enjoyment   employment

_____   _____   _____

Now use each word in a sentence.

1. _____

2. _____

3. _____

Pages 12-13 Write the word as directed.

cardboard

_____   (without vowels)

_____   (without consonants)

_____   (backwards)

_____   (correctly)

Pages 14-15 Look on page 14 and write three more **er** words, three more **ir** words, and three more **ur** words.

perfect   thirsty   furniture

_____   _____   _____

_____   _____   _____

_____   _____   _____

Touchdown!

29 –18 –71– 4 – Hike! Write the letters **ou** or **ow** to make 20 words. Then write them in alphabetical order. If you correctly alphabetize on all 20 "yard lines," you have scored a TD!

ABC Order
Yard lines

1. dr __ __ sy
2. __ __ tdoors
3. fr __ __ n
4. p __ __ er
5. m __ __ ntain
6. c __ __ nt
7. cr __ __ d
8. t __ __ chd __ __ n
9. r __ __ nded
10. p __ __ nd

1. _____
2. _____
3. _____
4. _____
5. _____
6. _____
7. _____
8. _____
9. _____
10. _____

Half-time!

11. sc __ __ t
12. undergr __ __ nd
13. t __ __ nh __ __ se
14. pr __ __ d
15. c __ __ nty
16. al __ __ d
17. b __ __ nce
18. gr __ __ nded
19. all __ __ ed
20. s __ __ nd

11. _____
12. _____
13. _____
14. _____
15. _____
16. _____
17. _____
18. _____
19. _____
20. _____

Oh, no! Crazy Larry ran the football backwards 99 yards and scored a touchdown for the **other** team! Can you write these backward spelling words correctly?

1. tnuoc _____
2. dednuor _____
3. dewolla _____
4. nwodhcuot _____
5. duorp _____
6. duola _____
7. dnuorgrednu _____
8. ytnuoc _____
9. dednuorg _____
10. dnuos _____
11. niatnuom _____
12. ysword _____
13. nworf _____
14. ecnuob _____
15. sroodtuo _____
16. tuocs _____
17. esuohnwot _____
18. rewop _____
19. dworc _____
20. dnuop _____

Capture the Doctor!

Paging Dr. Spellwell! These word patients are all mixed-up and on the wrong floors. Write each word on the correct floor.

"er" Floor	"ure" Floor	"or" Floor
(5 patients)		
	(6 patients)	
		(9 patients)

Dr. Spellwell's Patients

janitor	flavor
capture	finger
danger	nature
teacher	motor
refrigerator	radiator
bother	monitor
doctor	picture
pasture	feature
humor	creature
visitor	weather

a	b	c	d	e	f	g	h	i	j	k	l	m	n
H	R	F	O	K	S	N	X	A	W	Q	Y	C	V

o	p	q	r	s	t	u	v	w	x	y	z
L	D	J	G	I	P	T	B	Z	M	U	E

Use the code above to identify these "patients" of Dr. Spellwell. Write the words.

1. XTCLG   _____
2. FGKHPTGK   _____
3. CLVAPLG   _____
4. OHVNKG   _____
5. GKSGANKGHPLG   _____
6. VHPTGK   _____
7. SYHBLG   _____
8. RLPXKG   _____
9. WHVAPLG   _____
10. DAFPTGK   _____
11. CLPLG   _____
12. ZKHPXKG   _____
13. FHDPTGK   _____
14. OLFPLG   _____
15. SAVNKG   _____
16. SKHPTGK   _____
17. GHOAHPLG   _____
18. DHIPTGK   _____
19. BAIAPLG   _____
20. PKHFXKG   _____

The Awesome Saucer

Use the clues to unscramble the letters.
Write each word on the launch pad (line).
Try not to refer to the Word List on page 23.

1. That toaster DRCO is badly frayed. _____
2. The TURAHO is the person who wrote the book.

   _____
3. The button was RONT off my shirt! _____
4. The McCoys had two sons and one HADETUGR.

   _____
5. It's easier to drink with a WARTS. _____
6. You have an TROPIMNAT message waiting.

   _____
7. My dad is a blood ROOND. _____
8. The cup broke but not the CRAUSE. _____
9. A WHAK has excellent eyesight. _____
10. My zipper was HUGTAC in my jacket. _____
11. We have a fence around our front WALN. _____
12. People laugh SUBCEEA they're happy. _____
13. A ORFSET is a synonym of woods. _____
14. My smart sister is an ORNOH student. _____
15. Fluorescent colors are totally WAMOSEE! _____
16. The RATESOG shed is behind the garage. _____
17. Whose LATUF was it? _____
18. I think spinach tastes WUFLA! _____
19. GRINMON is my best time of day. _____
20. Her skirt had a FOLLAR pattern. _____

Using the Word List, follow these directions to write the correct words. **Hint:** Some words will be used more than once.

aw words

_____

_____

_____

_____

_____

or words with
1 syllable

_____

_____

or words with
2 syllables

_____

_____

_____

_____

_____

_____

_____

or word with the
most syllables

_____

au words with 1 syllable

_____

_____

au words with
2 syllables

_____

_____

_____

_____

words ending with **or**

_____

_____

_____

Extraterrestrial Word List

important	hawk	lawn
daughter	fault	honor
awesome	torn	forest
because	awful	donor
morning	floral	straw
storage	caught	cord
saucer	author	

The Curious Bulldog

Can you help Brutus the bulldog find the right /yo͝o/ and /o͝o/ words to fit in these boxes? He heard you are "dog-gone" good at it!

1.
2.
3.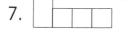
4.
5.
6.
7.
8.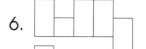
9.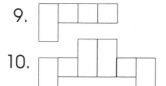
10.

11.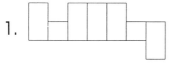
12.
13.
14.
15.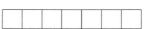
16.
17.
18.
19.
20.

The "Bull Pen" Word List

pulley	wooden	wolf	lure	during
furious	cookies	pure	fully	endure
fullest	bulldog	sure	stood	crooked
tourist	pushed	cure	curious	overture

IF0146 Spelling

"Bone up" on your words by following these clues.
Write . . .

1. a compound word. _____
2. words that can be used as verbs.

_____   _____   _____

_____   _____

3. four 1-syllable rhyming words. _____

_____   _____   _____

4. four words that begin with the letter C. _____

_____   _____   _____

5. a 3-syllable word that begins with the letter O.
_____

6. two words that begin with consonant blends.
_____   _____

7. four **oo** words. _____   _____

_____   _____

8. Ten /**yŏo**/ words   Ten /**ŏŏ**/ words

_____   _____

_____   _____

_____   _____

_____   _____

_____   _____

_____   _____

_____   _____

_____   _____

_____   _____

_____   _____

Haunted!

The vowel pairs have mysteriously disappeared from these words. Use the haunted house decoder to break the code and write these words.

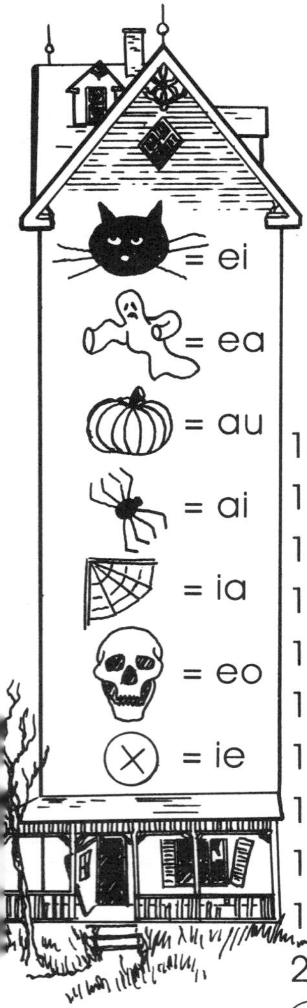

= ei
= ea
= au
= ai
= ia
= eo
= ie

1. d ___ ry ________
2. h ___ lthy ________
3. ___ ghteen ________
4. pl ___ sant ________
5. v ___ n ________
6. br ___ th ________
7. l ___ ghing ________
8. br ___ d ________
9. w ___ rd ________
10. d ___ th ________
11. t ___ ght ________
12. n ___ ghborhood ________
13. d ___ ry ________
14. br ___ the ________
15. fr ___ ght ________
16. r ___ lly ________
17. l ___ pard ________
18. f ___ rce ________
19. p ___ rce ________
20. h ___ nted ________

How many ___ words? ________ ___ words? ________

___ words? ________ ___ words? ________

___ words? ________ ___ words? ________

___ words? ________

Cover page 26 before entering these haunted houses!
If you believe a Word List word is spelled correctly, write
it in the House of Wonders. If it is incorrect, write it **correctly** in the House of Horrors.

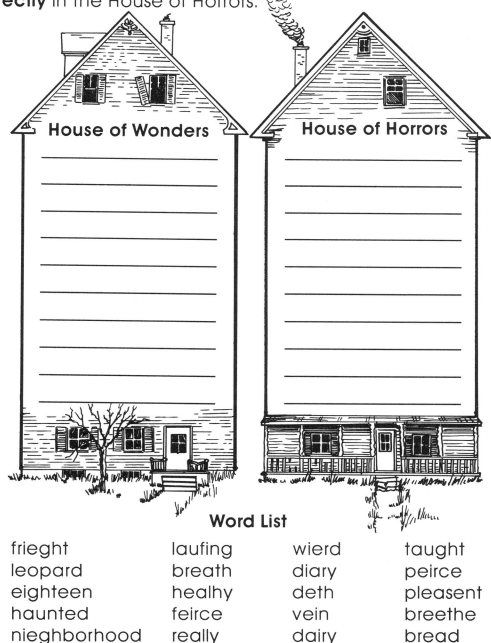

House of Wonders

House of Horrors

Word List

frieght	laufing	wierd	taught
leopard	breath	diary	peirce
eighteen	healhy	deth	pleasent
haunted	feirce	vein	breethe
nieghborhood	really	dairy	bread

Once upon a Button . . .

The / ə / sound is represented by a button in each of these words. Write the correct spelling and the number of syllables in each word.

		No. of Syllables
1. ⊙ ddition	_____	_____
2. muse ⊕ m	_____	_____
3. ✕ cross	_____	_____
4. bott ⊙ m	_____	_____
5. mis ✳ ry	_____	_____
6. ⊙ round	_____	_____
7. ✿ gree	_____	_____
8. purp ◇ se	_____	_____
9. festiv ◉ l	_____	_____
10. fam ⊘ ly	_____	_____
11. ⊙ ddress	_____	_____
12. par ✳ nt	_____	_____
13. ✳ pon	_____	_____
14. b ◉ nan ✕	_____	_____
15. ✕ bout	_____	_____
16. c ◉ llect	_____	_____
17. alph ◉ bet	_____	_____
18. lig ✳ ment	_____	_____
19. ✳ cad ✳ my	_____	_____
20. c ⊙ mmand	_____	_____

Word List

ligament	agree	upon	across	addition
command	academy	parent	misery	banana
museum	address	around	about	bottom
alphabet	purpose	festival	collect	family

Decode these / ə / words by writing the letter that comes **after** each letter given. The first one has been done for you.

1. TONM	=	<u>UPON</u>
2. ZANTS	=	_____
3. ANSSNL	=	_____
4. OTQONRD	=	_____
5. EDRSHUZK	=	_____
6. ZCCQDRR	=	_____
7. BNLLZMC	=	_____
8. LTRDTL	=	_____
9. AZMZMZ	=	_____
10. ZBQNRR	=	_____
11. ZCCHSHNM	=	_____
12. OZQDMS	=	_____
13. ZQNTMC	=	_____
14. ZFQDD	=	_____
15. BNKKDBS	=	_____
16. EZLHKX	=	_____
17. ZKOGZADS	=	_____
18. ZBZCDLX	=	_____
19. KHFZLDMS	=	_____
20. LHRDQX	=	_____

Now, write your name in this code.

_____

Somewhere Out There

"Somewhere" there is an **air** word in each group of letters. Beginning with the first letter, cross out every other letter. Write the remaining letters on the line.

1. s̸h̸e̸a̸i̸r̸   <u>hair</u>
2. lsopialroe   _____
3. barniytwehaesrie   _____
4. spoeratr   _____
5. twehaerrpe   _____
6. agoleanrse   _____
7. sporeenplanroe   _____
8. wanraela   _____
9. curposotranilres   _____
10. omoatree   _____
11. astolmrebwohiesrwe   _____
12. twieralr   _____
13. garilropuleasnoe   _____
14. emoasrerly   _____
15. odiasrmeldresvoill   _____
16. esoctauricre   _____
17. surnofeamivr   _____
18. isotwanrre   _____
19. griefpoanier   _____
20. afaloasinr   _____

CHALLENGE: Write a secret message to a friend or family member using this code.

Write the words from page 30 that fit each description.

ar spellings of **/air/**

_____
_____
_____
_____
_____
_____
_____
_____

air spellings of **/air/**

_____
_____
_____
_____
_____

ear spellings of /**air**/

_____
_____

3-syllable words

_____
_____

er spellings of /**air**/

_____
_____

1-syllable words

_____
_____
_____

2-syllable words

_____
_____
_____
_____
_____
_____

_____
_____
_____
_____
_____
_____

Weird Cereal!

Snap, crackle, and spell these /**ear**/ words
by using the "Weird - O Spoon Decoder."

	A	B	C	D	E	F	G	H	I	J	K	L	M
	4	16	6	9	1	13	19	25	3	17	23	8	21
	10	5	15	24	7	2	20	12	18	14	26	11	22
	N	O	P	Q	R	S	T	U	V	W	X	Y	Z

1. 9 – 3 – 2 – 4 – 15 – 15 – 1 – 4 –7 _____
2. 20 – 1 – 4 – 7 _____
3. 15 – 3 – 1 – 7 _____
4. 2 – 3 – 10 – 6 – 1 – 7 – 1 – 8 –11 _____
5. 6 – 4 – 7 – 1 – 1 – 7 _____
6. 16 –1 – 4 – 7 – 9 _____
7. 20 – 1 – 4 – 7 – 11 _____
8. 6 – 25 – 1 – 1 – 7 _____
9. 17 – 1 – 1 – 7 _____
10. 21 – 3 – 7 – 7 – 5 – 7 _____
11. 9 – 1 – 4 – 7 _____
12. 14 – 1 – 3 – 7 – 9 _____
13. 14 – 1 – 4 – 7 – 11 _____
14. 13 – 1 – 4 – 7 _____
15. 2 – 20 – 1 – 1 – 7 _____
16. 15 – 1 – 7 – 3 – 5 – 9 _____
17. 20 – 3 – 1 – 7 _____
18. 21 – 1 – 7 – 1 _____
19. 6 – 1 – 7 – 1 – 4 – 8 _____
20. 11 – 1 – 4 – 7 – 8 – 11 _____

Spoons up and ready! Write the word for each clue. Use the Word List or challenge yourself by covering the previous page. Dig in!

1. part of a letter's closure _____
2. eyes filled with drops of water _____
3. cattle _____
4. dock _____
5. a job or life's work _____
6. a punctuation mark _____
7. to yell for a team _____
8. layer _____
9. vanish _____
10. tired _____
11. to heckle, make fun of _____
12. once a year _____
13. very strange _____
14. breakfast grains _____
15. slightest amount _____
16. part of a letter's greeting _____
17. a drop of water from the eye _____
18. afraid of _____
19. looking glass _____
20. chin hair _____

Review

Pages 18-19 Write **one** sentence using all three words.

underground   mountain   allowed

_____

_____

Pages 20-21 Write each word. Then, for each clue in parentheses find a word on page 20 with the same **or, ure** or **er** spelling.

visitor   creature   weather

_____   _____   _____

(12-letter word)   (to seize)   (warning)

Pages 22-23 Write each word in the correct word box. Then rewrite it again under its word box.

daughter   important   awesome

_____   _____   _____

Pages 24-25 Write the words in ABC order.

curious   _____

during   _____

crooked   _____

Pages 26-27   Write each word according to directions.

pleasant   fierce   neighborhood

Without Vowels		**Without Consonants**	
frc	_____	eiooo	_____
nghbrhd	_____	eaa	_____
plsnt	_____	iee	_____

Pages 28-29   Make word lists by writing a word beginning with each of the following letters.

Ex: A _unt_____   P _____   A _____
      D _og_____   U _____   C _____
      D _____ R _____   A _____
      R _____ P _____   D _____
      E _____ O _____   E _____
      S _____ S _____   M _____
      S _____ E _____   Y _____

Pages 30-31   Using your own paper, make spelling
pyramids for these words.

somewhere   **Example:** spare   s
prepare   sp
daredevil   spa
scarce   spar
airplane   spare

Pages 32-33   Fill in the correct word.

cereal   1. She plans a _____ in medicine.
sincerely 2. _____ is made from grains.
career   3. The letter was signed, "_____ yours."

Smiling Sneakers

On your mark! Get set! . . . Choose a consonant blend for each group of letters. Then write the word. . . . Go!

1. __ __ iling _____
2. __ __ easure _____
3. __ __ eleton _____
4. __ __ imbing _____
5. __ __ oser _____
6. __ __ ift _____
7. __ __ ait _____
8. __ __ azed _____
9. __ __ ooth _____
10. __ __ arl _____
11. __ __ eaver _____
12. __ __ ames _____
13. __ __ our _____
14. __ __ obe _____
15. __ __ ateboard _____
16. __ __ acier _____
17. __ __ eater _____
18. __ __ irling _____
19. __ __ othing _____
20. __ __ eptical _____

cl
sm
sk
sn
fl
tr
sw
gl

If the sneakers were racing, which one would win for having the most words? _____

Answer Key

Spelling
Homework Booklet
Grade 4

The short vowels a, e, i, o and u have disappeared into the air! Add vowels to make words from the following letters. Write each word on the line.

1. k_i_tch_e_n — *kitchen*
2. v_e_g_e_table — *vegetable*
3. h_o_sp_i_tal — *hospital*
4. r_e_ct_a_ngle — *rectangle*
5. sk_e_l_e_t_o_n — *skeleton*
6. j_a_n_i_tor — *janitor*
7. b_o_bsl_e_d — *bobsled*
8. cl_o_s_e_t — *closet*
9. ut_e_ns_i_l — *utensil*
10. _o_ctop_u_s — *octopus*
11. cuc_u_mber — *cucumber*
12. sh_a_mr_o_ck — *shamrock*
13. s_u_dd_e_n — *sudden*
14. f_i_n_i_sh — *finish*
15. p_u_pp_e_t — *puppet*
16. c_a_nt_a_loupe — *cantaloupe*
17. f_a_nt_a_sy — *fantasy*
18. b_a_tht_u_b — *bathtub*
19. pr_i_nc_i_p_a_l — *principal*
20. ch_i_ck_e_n — *chicken*

©1992 Instructional Fair, Inc.   2   IF0146 Spelling

The prince has changed the station on his boom box. Now the consonants have disappeared. Fill in the blanks with words from page 2, and then write each word on the line.

1. o_c_to_pu_s — *octopus*
2. ba_th_tub — *bathtub*
3. ho_s_pi_t_al — *hospital*
4. re_c_ta_ng_le — *rectangle*
5. ute_n_si_l_ — *utensil*
6. f_an_ta_sy_ — *fantasy*
7. _s_ke_l_e_to_n — *skeleton*
8. _j_ani_t_o_r_ — *janitor*
9. _s_udde_n_ — *sudden*
10. p_u_ppe_t_ — *puppet*
11. pr_in_ci_p_al — *principal*
12. _c_an_t_alou_p_e — *cantaloupe*
13. c_h_ic_k_en — *chicken*
14. _c_u_c_umber — *cucumber*
15. bo_b_sl_e_d — *bobsled*
16. c_l_o_s_et — *closet*
17. _s_ha_m_ro_c_k — *shamrock*
18. _f_in_i_sh — *finish*
19. v_e_g_e_ta_b_le — *vegetable*
20. ki_t_c_h_en — *kitchen*

©1992 Instructional Fair, Inc.   3   IF0146 Spelling

Computers to the Rescue!

Enter the words on the computer screen into the correct data bank by writing them on the lines.

Word List

huge	jungle	pumpkin
used	fudge	thunder	avenue
trust	lucky	human	mustard
tune	hung	public	beauty
until	museum	rescue	computer

yōō Data Bank
- *huge*
- *used*
- *tune*
- *hue*
- *museum*
- *human*
- *rescue*
- *avenue*
- *beauty*
- *computer*

ŭ Data Bank
- *trust*
- *until*
- *fudge*
- *lucky*
- *hung*
- *jungle*
- *thunder*
- *public*
- *pumpkin*
- *mustard*

©1992 Instructional Fair, Inc.   4   IF0146 Spelling

Circle the misspelled words in each sentence. Write the words correctly on the lines. **Challenge:** Try it without looking at the previous page.

1. I like (mustard) on my hotdog. *mustard*
2. There is a (hudge) dog that lives on Grant (Avenu.) *huge* *Avenue*
3. The show was on (publik) television. *public*
4. (Rescu) 911 is on TV on Tuesday night. *Rescue*
5. Tim loves (punkin) pie and peanut butter (huge.) *pumpkin* *fudge*
6. You can always (tust) a good friend. *trust*
7. The (muzeum) was painted a brownish (hew.) *museum* *hue*
8. Lightning and (thundder) came with the storm in the (jungel.) *thunder* *jungle*
9. That (hunam) being's (beuty) is more than skin-deep. *human* *beauty*
10. The seatbelt (hunng) out of our (yused) car. *hung* *used*
11. We can play a (fun) on our (cumputor.) *tune* *computer*
12. We are (luky) because we can stay up (untill) 10:30. *lucky* *until*

©1992 Instructional Fair, Inc.   5   IF0146 Spelling

Aviator Hotel

"Fly" these ā and ō words from the Aviator Hotel to the correct landing strip by writing them in alphabetical order. Fasten your seat belts!

Word List

ocean, aviator, chose, crazy, total, station, protection, favorite, zero, create, below, follow, laser, elevator, almost, alligator, hotel, parade, program, weight

ā Landing Strip
1. *alligator* 6. *favorite*
2. *aviator* 7. *laser*
3. *crazy* 8. *parade*
4. *create* 9. *station*
5. *elevator* 10. *weight*

ō Landing Strip
1. *almost* 6. *ocean*
2. *below* 7. *program*
3. *chose* 8. *protection*
4. *follow* 9. *total*
5. *hotel* 10. *zero*

©1992 Instructional Fair, Inc.   6   IF0146 Spelling

Here is your flight plan, Spelling Aviator! Write the correct word by each clue. Earn your wings if you can do it correctly without using the Word List on page 6.

1. a beam of light — *laser*
2. safety — *protection*
3. not quite — *almost*
4. first choice — *favorite*
5. for overnights — *hotel*
6. less than one — *zero*
7. a show — *program*
8. opposite of above — *below*
9. a bus, train, radio or TV... — *station*
10. floats, bands — *parade*
11. 94 pounds — *weight*
12. the sea — *ocean*
13. picked — *chose*
14. all of something — *total*
15. a flyer — *aviator*
16. zany — *crazy*
17. a reptile — *alligator*
18. to invent — *create*
19. tag along behind — *follow*
20. "Going Up!" — *elevator*

©1992 Instructional Fair, Inc.   7   IF0146 Spelling

The Secret Pirate

Ahoy, Matey! Fill in the missing letters of these ē and ī words. Write the boxed letters on the lines below to find the name of a famous pirate.

Word List

ceiling, supply, either, motorcycle, female, pirate, meteor, deny, chief, surprise, idea, reply, secret, lying, peanuts, behind, greeting, awhile, bicycle, believe

1. m_e_t_e_o_r — *meteor*
2. p_e_a_n_u_ts — *peanuts*
3. r_e_p_l_y — *reply*
4. ch_i_e_f — *chief*
5. b_i_c_y_c_l_e — *bicycle*
6. c_e_i_l_i_n_g — *ceiling*
7. s_u_p_p_l_y — *supply*
8. d_e_n_y — *deny*
9. f_e_m_a_l_e — *female*
10. e_i_th_e_r — *either*
11. p_i_r_a_t_e — *pirate*
12. i_d_e_a — *idea*
13. b_e_h_i_nd — *behind*
14. s_u_r_p_r_i_s_e — *surprise*
15. l_y_i_ng — *lying*
16. m_o_t_o_r_c_y_c_l_e — *motorcycle*
17. s_e_c_r_e_t — *secret*
18. g_r_e_e_t_i_n_g — *greeting*
19. a_w_h_i_l_e — *awhile*
20. b_e_l_i_e_v_e — *believe*

L o n g   J o h n   S i l v e r
15 1 2 5   16 13 18   14 4 19 20 8 10

©1992 Instructional Fair, Inc.   8   IF0146 Spelling

Page 9 — Wordsearch

Use the Word List to complete this wordsearch. The words will be across, down or backwards. The ship's gold is yours if you can also find the "secret pirate's" name!

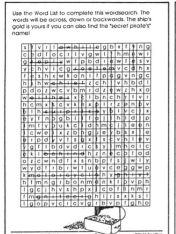

A Royal Appointment

Hear Ye! Hear Ye! You have an appointment with the king to unscramble these royal words. Write them on the lines, with a regal flourish, of course!

1. covie — *voice*
2. pintemaptno — *appointment*
3. soyin — *noisy*
4. talyyol — *loyalty*
5. lofi — *foil*
6. ommelpnety — *employment*
7. ijando — *adjoin*
8. davio — *avoid*
9. mytenjone — *enjoyment*
10. lorib — *broil*
11. noij — *join*
12. potsadinip — *disappoint*
13. polis — *spoil*
14. yolar — *royal*
15. foyluj — *joyful*
16. yanno — *annoy*
17. stomi — *moist*
18. tinjo — *joint*
19. liibong — *boiling*
20. cohcie — *choice*

Royal Word List

appointment	spoil	loyalty
employment	broil	royal
disappoint	foil	moist
enjoyment	join	voice
choice	joint	boiling
		adjoin
		avoid
		joyful
		noisy

Page 11

Proclaim the royal syllables! Find and write the words to fulfill your royal spelling duties.

oy – 2 syllables	oy – 3 syllables
annoy	*enjoyment*
joyful	*employment*
royal	*loyalty*

oi – 1 syllable	oi – 2 syllables
voice	*avoid*
spoil	*noisy*
join	*adjoin*
joint	*boiling*
choice	
foil	
moist	oi – 3 syllables
broil	*appointment*
	disappoint

The Sparkler Party

A	B	C	D	E	F	G	H	I	J	K	L	M
21	22	23	24	25	26	1	2	3	4	5	6	7

N	O	P	Q	R	S	T	U	V	W	X	Y	Z
8	9	10	11	12	13	14	15	16	17	18	19	20

Use the code to write these /är/ words. Finding all 20 words earns you an invitation to the "Sparkler Party"!

1. 22–21–12–1–25 — *barge*
2. 1–21–12–24–25–8 — *garden*
3. 13–10–21–12–5–6–25 — *sparkler*
4. 23–21–12–1–9 — *cargo*
5. 13–14–21–12–14 — *start*
6. 21–12–7–9 — *army*
7. 2–21–12–7–6–25–13–13 — *harmless*
8. 23–21–12–8–3–16–21–6 — *carnival*
9. 1–21–12–22–21–1–25 — *garbage*
10. 19–21–12–24 — *yard*
11. 23–21–12–24–22–9–21–12–24 — *cardboard*
12. 2–21–12–24–6–19 — *hardly*
13. 22–21–12–22–25–12 — *barber*
14. 10–21–12–14–19 — *party*
15. 13–23–21–12–26 — *scarf*
16. 13–2–21–12–5 — *shark*
17. 24–21–12–5–8–25–13–13 — *darkness*
18. 23–21–12–10–25–14 — *carpet*
19. 2–21–12–8–25–13–13 — *harness*
20. 7–21–12–22–6–25–13 — *marbles*

Join the party!

Join the party! Use words from page 12 to fill in the blanks.

1. We grew onions and corn in our *garden*.
2. Mom's *scarf* matched her blouse.
3. They watched *harness* racing at the fair.
4. The *Army* and Air Force fought in the desert.
5. We brought kittens home in a *cardboard* box.
6. I could *hardly* believe my eyes!
7. The *barge* carried coal down the river.
8. A *Carnival* is similar to a fair.
9. It was hard to see in the *darkness* of the cave.
10. She had a *party* for her eleventh birthday.
11. My mom plants many flowers in our *yard*.
12. A *shark* warning was posted at the beach.
13. Gentlemen, *start* your engines!
14. Bob bought a Fourth of July *sparkler*.
15. Do you recycle your *garbage*?
16. Most spiders are *harmless* to humans.
17. The ship's *cargo* was headed for Canada.
18. The family room had brand-new *carpet*.
19. My dad and I go to the same *barber* for haircuts.
20. Do you know how to shoot *marbles*?

How many did you get correct? _____

(17 – 20) You're a sparkler! (7–11) You fizzled out!
(12 – 16) A real fireball! (0 – 6) • A dud! Try again!

The Perfect Shirt

Write the er, ir and ur words on the correct T-shirt. Trace over the letters er in purple, ir in red and ur in yellow. Design and color sleeves to create a perfect shirt!

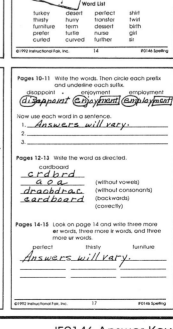

er: *transfer, perfect, desert, prefer, dessert, term*

ur: *turkey, hurry, curved, turtle, furniture, nurse, further, curled*

ir: *girl, thirsty, birth, shirt, twirl, sir*

Word List

turkey	desert	perfect	shirt
thirsty	hurry	transfer	twirl
furniture	term	dessert	birth
prefer	turtle	nurse	girl
curled	curved	further	sir

Page 15 — Crossword

Across
2. medical helper — *nurse*
6. not straight — *curved*
7. would rather have — *prefer*
9. exchange — *transfer*
11. item of clothing — *shirt*
12. hard-shelled animal — *turtle*
13. beyond — *further*
17. spin around — *twirl*
19. rolled into a ball — *curled*
20. Thanksgiving fowl — *turkey*

Down
1. Ideal — *perfect*
3. act of being born — *birth*
4. tables, chairs, sofas — *furniture*
5. sandy area — *desert*
8. cake, pie, cookie — *dessert*
10. term of respect — *sir*
14. needing to drink — *thirsty*
15. female — *girl*
16. rush — *hurry*
18. period of time — *term*

Review

Pages 2-3 Circle the ĕ and ĭ vowels.

rĕctangle | kĭtchen
pŭddĭng | chĭcken
skĕleton | utĕnsil

Pages 4-5 Fill in the correct word.

rescue
beauty
computer

1. That horse is a *beauty*.
2. The printer on our *computer* doesn't work.
3. John will *rescue* the kitten.

Look up and write four more ū words. Use these in sentences on another paper. *Answers will vary.*

Pages 6-7 Fill in the boxes with the correct letters. Write these words in alphabetical order.

favorite — *ocean* — *create*
create — *favorite* — *favorite*
ocean — *create* — *ocean*

Pages 8-9 Make word pyramids for these words on another sheet of paper.

believe
surprise
chief

Example: deny
d
de
den
deny

Pages 10-11

Pages 10-11 Write the words. Then circle each prefix and underline each suffix.

disappoint • enjoyment • employment
disappoint *enjoyment* *employment*

Now use each word in a sentence. *Answers will vary.*

1. _____
2. _____
3. _____

Pages 12-13 Write the word as directed.

cardboard
crdbrd (without vowels)
aoa (without consonants)
draobdrac (backwards)
cardboard (correctly)

Pages 14-15 Look on page 14 and write three more er words, three more ir words, and three more ur words.

perfect thirsty furniture
Answers will vary.

Touchdown!

29 – 18 – 71 – 4 – Hike! Write the letters ou or ow to make 20 words. Then write them in alphabetical order. If you correctly alphabetize on all 20 "yard lines," you have scored a TD!

ABC Order

Yard lines

1. dr _ow_ sy
2. _ou_ tdoors
3. fr _ow_ n
4. p _ow_ er
5. m _ou_ ntain
6. c _ou_ nt
7. cr _ow_ d
8. t _ou_ chd _ow_ n
9. r _ou_ nded
10. s _ou_ nd

1. _allowed_
2. _aloud_
3. _bounce_
4. _count_
5. _county_
6. _crowd_
7. _drowsy_
8. _frown_
9. _grounded_
10. _mountain_

Half-time!

11. sc _ou_ t
12. undergr _ou_ nd
13. t _ou_ wnh _ou_ se
14. pr _ou_ d
15. c _ou_ nty
16. al _ou_ d
17. b _ou_ nce
18. gr _ou_ nded
19. all _ow_ ed
20. s _ou_ nd

11. _outdoors_
12. _pound_
13. _power_
14. _proud_
15. _rounded_
16. _scout_
17. _sound_
18. _touchdown_
19. _townhouse_
20. _underground_

©1992 Instructional Fair, Inc. 18 IF0146 Spelling

Oh, no! Crazy Larry ran the football backwards 99 yards and scored a touchdown for the **other** team! Can you write these backward spelling words correctly?

1. tnuoc — _count_
2. dednuor — _rounded_
3. dewolla — _allowed_
4. nwodhcuot — _touchdown_
5. duorp — _proud_
6. duola — _aloud_
7. dnuorgrednu — _underground_
8. ytnuoc — _county_
9. dednuorg — _grounded_
10. dnuos — _sound_
11. niatnuom — _mountain_
12. ysword — _drowsy_
13. nworf — _frown_
14. ecnuob — _bounce_
15. sroodtuo — _outdoors_
16. tuocs — _scout_
17. esuohnwot — _townhouse_
18. rewop — _power_
19. dworc — _crowd_
20. dnuop — _pound_

©1992 Instructional Fair, Inc. 19 IF0146 Spelling

Capture the Doctor!

Paging Dr. Spellwell! These word patients are all mixed-up and on the wrong floors. Write each word on the correct floor.

"er" Floor	"ure" Floor	"or" Floor
bother	_picture_	_janitor_
finger	_capture_	_monitor_
danger	_nature_	_doctor_
teacher	_pasture_	_flavor_
weather	_creature_	_radiator_
(5 patients)	_feature_	_motor_
	(6 patients)	_refrigerator_
		humor
		visitor
		(9 patients)

Dr. Spellwell's Patients

janitor, flavor, capture, finger, danger, nature, teacher, motor, refrigerator, radiator, bother, monitor, doctor, picture, pasture, feature, humor, creature, visitor, weather

©1992 Instructional Fair, Inc. 20 IF0146 Spelling

---

a b c d e f g h i j k l m n
H R F O K S N X A W Q Y C V

o p q r s t u v w x y z
L D J G I P T B Z M U E

Use the code above to identify these "patients" of Dr. Spellwell. Write the words.

1. XTCLG — _humor_
2. FGKHPTGK — _creature_
3. CLVAPLG — _monitor_
4. OHVNKG — _danger_
5. GKSGANKGHPLG — _refrigerator_
6. VHPTGK — _nature_
7. SYHBLG — _flavor_
8. RLPXKG — _bother_
9. WHVAPLG — _janitor_
10. DAFPTGK — _picture_
11. CLPLG — _motor_
12. ZKHPXKG — _weather_
13. FHDPTGK — _capture_
14. OLFPLG — _doctor_
15. SAVNKG — _finger_
16. SKHPTGK — _feature_
17. GHOAHPLG — _radiator_
18. DHIPTGK — _pasture_
19. BAIAPLG — _visitor_
20. PKHFXKG — _teacher_

©1992 Instructional Fair, Inc. 21 IF0146 Spelling

The Awesome Saucer

Use the clues to unscramble the letters. Write each word on the launch pad (line). Try not to refer to the Word List on page 23.

1. That toaster DRCO is badly frayed. — _cord_
2. The TURAHO is the person who wrote the book. — _author_
3. The button was RONT off my shirt! — _torn_
4. The McCoys had two sons and one HADETUGR. — _daughter_
5. It's easier to drink with a WARTS. — _straw_
6. You have an TROPIMNAT message waiting. — _important_
7. My dad is a blood ROOND. — _donor_
8. The cup broke but not the CRAUSE. — _saucer_
9. A WHAK has excellent eyesight. — _hawk_
10. My zipper was HUGTAC in my jacket. — _caught_
11. We have a fence around our front WALN. — _lawn_
12. People laugh SUBCEEA they're happy. — _because_
13. A ORFSET is a synonym of woods. — _forest_
14. My smart sister is an ORNOH student. — _honor_
15. Fluorescent colors are totally WAMOSEEI — _awesome_
16. The RATESOG shed is behind the garage. — _storage_
17. Whose LATUF was it? — _fault_
18. I think spinach tastes WUFLAI — _awful_
19. GRINMON is the best time of day. — _morning_
20. Her skirt had a FOLLAR pattern. — _floral_

©1992 Instructional Fair, Inc. 22 IF0146 Spelling

Using the Word List, follow these directions to write the correct words. **Hint:** Some words will be used more than once.

aw words	au words with 1 syllable
awful	_caught_
lawn	_fault_
straw	
awesome	**au words with 2 syllables**
hawk	_daughter_
	saucer
or words with 1 syllable	_because_
cord	_author_
torn	
	words ending with or
or words with 2 syllables	_author_
author	_honor_
honor	_donor_
storage	
forest	
donor	**Extraterrestrial Word List**
floral	important, hawk, lawn
morning	daughter, fault, honor
	awesome, torn, forest
or word with the most syllables	because, awful, donor
important	morning, floral, straw
	storage, caught, cord
	saucer, author

©1992 Instructional Fair, Inc. 23 IF0146 Spelling

The Curious Bulldog

Can you help Brutus the bulldog find the right /yoo/ and /oo/ words to fit in these boxes? He heard you are "dog-gone" good at it!

1. _bulldog_
2. _sure_
3. _furious_
4. _overture_
5. _wolf_
6. _fully_
7. _lure_
8. _fullest_
9. _pure_
10. _pulley_
11. _wooden_
12. _pushed_
13. _endure_
14. _during_
15. _stood_
16. _cure_
17. _cookies_
18. _tourist_
19. _curious_
20. _crooked_

The "Bull Pen" Word List

pulley	wooden	wolf	lure	during
furious	cookies	pure	fully	endure
fullest	bulldog	sure	stood	crooked
tourist	pushed	cure	curious	overture

©1992 Instructional Fair, Inc. 24 IF0146 Spelling

"Bone up" on your words by following these clues. Write . . .

1. a compound word. _bulldog_
2. words that can be used as verbs. _pushed_ _lure_ _cure_ _endure_ _stood_
3. four 1-syllable rhyming words. _cure_ _lure_ _pure_ _sure_
4. four words that begin with the letter C. _cure_ _cookies_ _crooked_ _curious_
5. a 3-syllable word that begins with the letter O. _overture_
6. two words that begin with consonant blends. _stood_ _crooked_
7. four oo words. _cookies_ _crooked_ _wooden_ _stood_
8. Ten /yoo/ words / Ten /oo/ words

Ten /yoo/ words	Ten /oo/ words
cure	_wolf_
lure	_wooden_
pure	_fully_
sure	_stood_
curious	_pulley_
tourist	_cookies_
furious	_bulldog_
endure	_pushed_
overture	_crooked_
during	_fullest_

©1992 Instructional Fair, Inc. 25 IF0146 Spelling

Haunted!

The vowel pairs have mysteriously disappeared from these words. Use the haunted house decoder to break the code and write these words.

1. d ⊗ ry — _diary_
2. h ⊕ lthy — _healthy_
3. ⊗ ghteen — _eighteen_
4. pl ⊗ sant — _pleasant_
5. v ⊗ n — _vein_
6. br ⊕ th — _breath_
7. l ⊗ ghing — _laughing_
8. br ⊕ d — _bread_
9. w ⊗ rd — _weird_
10. d ⊕ th — _death_
11. t ⊗ ght — _taught_
12. n ⊗ ghborhood — _neighborhood_
13. d ⊗ ry — _dairy_
14. br ⊕ the — _breathe_
15. fr ⊗ ght — _freight_
16. r ⊗ lly — _really_
17. l ⊕ pard — _leopard_
18. f ⊗ rce — _fierce_
19. p ⊗ rce — _pierce_
20. h ⊕ nted — _haunted_

decoder	
⊗ = ei	
⊕ = ea	
⊗ = au	
⊗ = ai	
⊗ = ia	
⊕ = eo	
⊗ = ie	

How many ⊗ words? _2_ words? _1_
words? _5_ words? _7_
words? _1_ words? _3_
words? _1_

©1992 Instructional Fair, Inc. 26 IF0146 Spelling

IF0146 Answer Key

Page 27

Cover page 26 before entering these haunted houses! If you believe a Word List word is spelled correctly, write it in the House of Wonders. If it is incorrect, write it **correctly** in the House of Horrors.

House of Wonders
leopard
eighteen
haunted
breath
really
diary
vein
dairy
taught
bread

House of Horrors
freight
neighborhood
laughing
healthy
fierce
weird
death
pierce
pleasant
breathe

Word List
frieght	laufing	wierd	taught
leopard	breath	diary	peirce
eighteen	healhy	deth	pleasent
haunted	feirce	vein	breethe
nieghborhood	really	dairy	bread

©1992 Instructional Fair, Inc.   27   IF0146 Spelling

Page 28

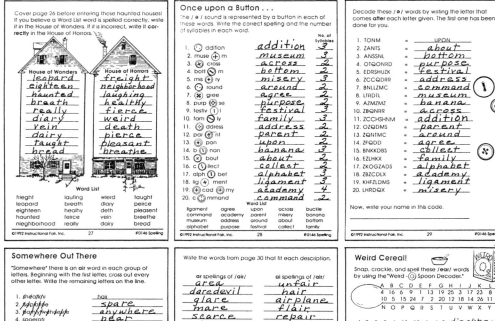

Once upon a Button . . .

The / ə / sound is represented by a button in each of these words. Write the correct spelling and the number of syllables in each word.

No. of Syllables

1. ⊙ ddition — addition — 3
2. muse ⊕ m — museum — 3
3. ⊛ cross — across — 2
4. bott ⊙ m — bottom — 2
5. mis ⊙ ry — misery — 3
6. ⊙ round — around — 2
7. ⊛ gree — agree — 2
8. purp ⊙ se — purpose — 2
9. festiv ① l — festival — 3
10. fam ⊙ ly — family — 3
11. ⊙ ddress — address — 2
12. par ⊕ nt — parent — 2
13. ⊕ pon — upon — 2
14. b ① nan — banana — 3
15. ⊙ bout — about — 2
16. c ① llect — collect — 2
17. alph ① bet — alphabet — 3
18. lig ⊕ ment — ligament — 3
19. ⊕ cad ⊕ my — academy — 4
20. c ⊙ mmand — command — 2

Word List
ligament	agree	upon	across	buckle
command	academy	parent	misery	banana
museum	address	around	about	bottom
alphabet	purpose	festival	collect	family

©1992 Instructional Fair, Inc.   28   IF0146 Spelling

Page 29

Decode these / ə / words by writing the letter that comes **after** each letter given. The first one is done for you.

1. TONM	=	UPON	
2. ZANTS	=	about	
3. ANSSNL	=	bottom	
4. OTQONRD	=	purpose	
5. EDRSHUZK	=	festival	
6. ZCCQDRR	=	address	
7. BNLLZMC	=	command	
8. LTRDTL	=	museum	
9. AZMZMZ	=	banana	
10. ZBQNRR	=	across	
11. ZCCHSHNM	=	addition	
12. OZQDMS	=	parent	
13. ZQNTMC	=	around	
14. ZFQDD	=	agree	
15. BNKKDBS	=	collect	
16. EZLHKX	=	family	
17. ZKOGZADS	=	alphabet	
18. ZBZCDLX	=	academy	
19. KHFZLDLMS	=	ligament	
20. LHRDQX	=	misery	

Now, write your name in this code.

©1992 Instructional Fair, Inc.   29   IF0146 Spelling

Page 30

Somewhere Out There

"Somewhere" there is an **air** word in each group of letters. Beginning with the first letter, cross out every other letter. Write the remaining letters on the line.

1. sheafight — hair
2. kspsaore — spare
3. panywwhheflrse — anywhere
4. spoerafr — pear
5. twehaerrpe — where
6. agolearre — glare
7. sporeenpianroe — prepare
8. wanraela — area
9. curposotranilres — upstairs
10. omaotree — mare
11. astoimrebwohiesrwe — somewhere
12. twierali — wear
13. garilropuleasnoe — airplane
14. emoasrerly — marry
15. odiasrmeldresvoill — daredevil
16. esoctlauricre — scarce
17. surnofeamivr — unfair
18. isotwanrre — stare
19. griefpoanier — repair
20. afaloasinr — flair

CHALLENGE: Write a secret message to a friend or family member using this code.

©1992 Instructional Fair, Inc.   30   IF0146 Spelling

Page 31

Write the words from page 30 that fit each description.

ar spellings of /air/
area
daredevil
glare
mare
scarce
spare
stare
marry
prepare

er spellings of /air/
where
somewhere
anywhere

2-syllable words
unfair
airplane
upstairs
marry
prepare
somewhere
repair

ai spellings of /air/
unfair
hair
airplane
flair
repair
upstairs

ear spellings of /air/
wear
pear

3-syllable words
daredevil
area
anywhere

1-syllable words
where
glare
mare
scarce
spare
stare
flair
wear
pear
hair

©1992 Instructional Fair, Inc.   31   IF0146 Spelling

Page 32

Weird Cereal!

Snap, crackle, and spell these /ear/ words by using the "Weird ⊙ Spoon Decoder."

A	B	C	D	E	F	G	H	I	J	K	L	M
4	16	6	9	1	13	19	25	3	17	23	8	21
10	5	15	24	7	2	20	12	18	14	26	11	22

| N | O | P | Q | R | S | T | U | V | W | X | Y | Z |

1. 9 – 3 – 2 – 4 – 15 – 15 – 1 – 4 – 7 — disappear
2. 20 – 1 – 4 – 7 — tear
3. 15 – 3 – 1 – 7 — pier
4. 2 – 3 – 10 – 6 – 1 – 7 – 1 – 8 – 11 — sincerely
5. 6 – 4 – 7 – 1 – 1 – 7 — career
6. 16 – 1 – 4 – 7 – 9 — beard
7. 20 – 1 – 4 – 7 – 11 — teary
8. 6 – 25 – 1 – 1 – 7 — cheer
9. 17 – 1 – 1 – 7 — jeer
10. 21 – 3 – 7 – 7 – 5 – 7 — mirror
11. 9 – 1 – 4 – 7 — dear
12. 14 – 1 – 3 – 7 – 9 — weird
13. 14 – 1 – 4 – 7 – 9 — weary
14. 13 – 1 – 4 – 7 — fear
15. 2 – 20 – 1 – 1 – 7 — steer
16. 15 – 1 – 7 – 3 – 5 – 9 — period
17. 20 – 3 – 1 – 7 — tier
18. 21 – 1 – 7 – 1 — mere
19. 6 – 1 – 7 – 1 – 4 – 8 — cereal
20. 11 – 1 – 4 – 7 – 8 – 11 — yearly

©1992 Instructional Fair, Inc.   32   IF0146 Spelling

Page 33

Spoons up and ready! Write the word for each clue. Use the Word List or challenge yourself by covering the previous page. Dig in!

1. part of a letter's closure — sincerely
2. eyes filled with drops of water — teary
3. cattle — steer
4. dock — pier
5. a job or life's work — career
6. a punctuation mark — period
7. to yell for a team — cheer
8. layer — tier
9. vanish — disappear
10. tired — weary
11. to heckle, make fun of — jeer
12. once a year — yearly
13. very strange — weird
14. breakfast grains — cereal
15. slightest amount — mere
16. part of a letter's greeting — dear
17. a drop of water from the eye — tear
18. afraid of — fear
19. looking glass — mirror
20. chin hair — beard

©1992 Instructional Fair, Inc.   33   IF0146 Spelling

Page 34

Review

Pages 18-19 Write **one** sentence using all three words.
underground   mountain   allowed
Answers will vary.

Pages 20-21 Write each word. Then, for each clue in parentheses find a word on page 20 with the same **or**, **ure** or **er** spelling.

visitor	creature	weather
visitor	creature	weather
refrigerator (12-letter word)	capture (to seize)	danger (warning)

Pages 22-23 Write each word in the correct word box. Then rewrite it again under its label.
daughter   important   awesome

awesome   daughter   important
awesome   daughter   important

Pages 24-25 Write the words in ABC order.
curious — crooked
during — curious
crooked — during

©1992 Instructional Fair, Inc.   34   IF0146 Spelling

Page 35

Pages 26-27 Write each word according to directions.
pleasant   fierce   neighborhood

	Without Vowels	**Without Consonants**
frc	fierce	eiooo — neighborhood
nghbrhd	neighborhood	eaa — pleasant
plsnt	pleasant	iee — fierce

Pages 28-29 Make word lists by writing a word beginning with each of the following letters.
Ex: A unt   P _____   A _____
D og   U _____   C _____
D _____   R _____
R _____   *Answers will vary.*
E _____   O _____   E _____
S _____   S _____   M _____
S _____   E _____   Y _____

Pages 30-31 Using your own paper, make spelling pyramids for these words.
somewhere   **Example:** spare   s
prepare   sp
daredevil   spa
scarce   spar
airplane   spare

Pages 32-33 Fill in the correct word.
cereal   1. She plans a career in medicine.
sincerely   2. Cereal is made from grains.
career   3. The letter was signed, "Sincerely yours."

©1992 Instructional Fair, Inc.   35   IF0146 Spelling

©1992 Instructional Fair, Inc.   IF0146 Answer Key

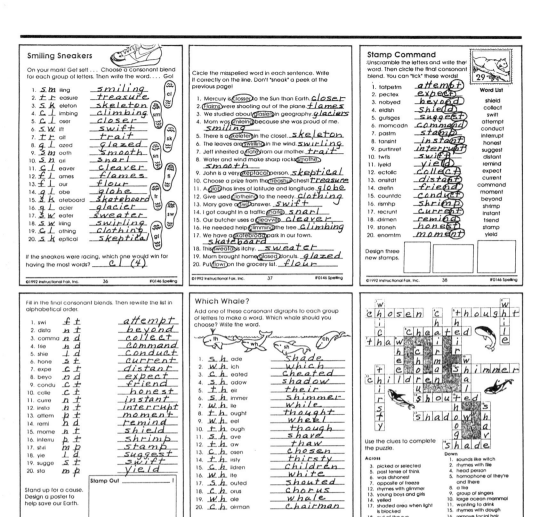

Smiling Sneakers

On your mark! Get set! . . . Choose a consonant blend for each group of letters. Then write the word. . . . Go!

1. _sm_ iling — smiling
2. _tr_ easure — treasure
3. _sk_ eleton — skeleton
4. _cl_ imbing — climbing
5. _cl_ oser — closer
6. _sw_ ift — swift
7. _tr_ ait — trait
8. _gl_ azed — glazed
9. _sm_ ooth — smooth
10. _sn_ arl — snarl
11. _cl_ eaver — cleaver
12. _fl_ ames — flames
13. _fl_ our — flour
14. _gl_ obe — globe
15. _sk_ ateboard — skateboard
16. _gl_ acier — glacier
17. _sw_ eater — sweater
18. _sw_ irling — swirling
19. _cl_ othing — clothing
20. _sk_ eptical — skeptical

If the sneakers were racing, which one would win for having the most words? __cl (4)__

Consonant blend labels (footprints): cl, sm, sk, sn, fl, tr, sw, gl

©1992 Instructional Fair, Inc.   36   IF0146 Spelling

Circle the misspelled word in each sentence. Write it correctly on the line. Don't "sneak" a peek at the previous page!

1. Mercury is closer to the Sun than Earth. closer
2. Flames were shooting out of the plane. flames
3. We studied about glaciers in geography. glaciers
4. Mom was smiling because she was proud of me. smiling
5. There is a skeleton in the closet. skeleton
6. The leaves are swirling in the wind. swirling
7. Jeff inherited a trait from our mother. trait
8. Water and wind make sharp rocks smooth. smooth
9. John is a very skeptical person. skeptical
10. Choose a prize from the treasure chest! treasure
11. A globe has lines of latitude and longitude. globe
12. Give used clothing to the needy. clothing
13. Mary gave a swift answer. swift
14. I got caught in a traffic snarl. snarl
15. Our butcher uses a cleaver. cleaver
16. He needed help climbing the tree. climbing
17. We have a skateboard park in our town. skateboard
18. This sweater is itchy. sweater
19. Mom brought home glazed donuts. glazed
20. Put flour on the grocery list. flour

©1992 Instructional Fair, Inc.   37   IF0146 Spelling

Stamp Command

Unscramble the letters and write the word. Then circle the final consonant blend. You can "lick" these words!

1. tatpetm — attempt
2. pectex — expect
3. nobyed — beyond
4. eldish — shield
5. gutsges — suggest
6. momcadn — command
7. pastm — stamp
8. tansint — instant
9. purtinret — interrupt
10. twfis — swift
11. lyeld — yield
12. ectollc — collect
13. ansitdt — distant
14. drefin — friend
15. countdc — conduct
16. rismhp — shrimp
17. recrunt — current
18. drimen — remind
19. stoneh — honest
20. enomtm — moment

Word List

shield
collect
swift
attempt
conduct
interrupt
honest
suggest
distant
remind
expect
current
command
moment
beyond
shrimp
instant
friend
stamp
yield

Design three new stamps.

©1992 Instructional Fair, Inc.   38   IF0146 Spelling

Fill in the final consonant blends. Then rewrite the list in alphabetical order.

1. swi _ft_ — attempt
2. dista _nt_ — beyond
3. comma _nd_ — collect
4. frie _nd_ — command
5. shie _ld_ — conduct
6. hone _st_ — current
7. expe _ct_ — distant
8. beyo _nd_ — expect
9. condu _ct_ — friend
10. colle _ct_ — honest
11. curre _nt_ — instant
12. insta _nt_ — interrupt
13. attem _pt_ — moment
14. remi _nd_ — remind
15. mome _nt_ — shield
16. interru _pt_ — shrimp
17. shri _mp_ — stamp
18. yie _ld_ — suggest
19. sugge _st_ — swift
20. sta _mp_ — yield

Stand up for a cause. Design a poster to help save our Earth.

Stamp Out _____ !

©1992 Instructional Fair, Inc.   39   IF0146 Spelling

Which Whale?

Add one of these consonant digraphs to each group of letters to make a word. Which whale should you choose? Write the word.

(whales: th, wh, sh, ch)

1. _sh_ ade — shade
2. _wh_ ich — which
3. _ch_ eated — cheated
4. _sh_ adow — shadow
5. _th_ eir — their
6. _sh_ immer — shimmer
7. _wh_ ile — while
8. _th_ ought — thought
9. _wh_ eel — wheel
10. _th_ ough — though
11. _sh_ ave — shave
12. _th_ aw — thaw
13. _ch_ osen — chosen
14. _th_ irsty — thirsty
15. _ch_ ildren — children
16. _wh_ ite — white
17. _sh_ outed — shouted
18. _ch_ orus — chorus
19. _wh_ ale — whale
20. _ch_ airman — chairman

©1992 Instructional Fair, Inc.   40   IF0146 Spelling

(crossword puzzle)

Use the clues to complete the puzzle.

Across
3. picked or selected
5. past tense of think
7. opposite of freeze
12. rhymes with glimmer
13. young boys and girls
14. yelled
17. shaded area when light is blocked
18. out of the sun

Down
1. sounds like witch
2. rhymes with file
4. head person
5. homophone of they're and there
6. a tire
9. group of singers
10. large ocean mammal
11. wanting to drink
15. rhymes with dough
16. remove facial hair

©1992 Instructional Fair, Inc.   41   IF0146 Spelling

Chill Out!

Decode each word and write it on the line. Keep cool; chill out; this is sno' easy!

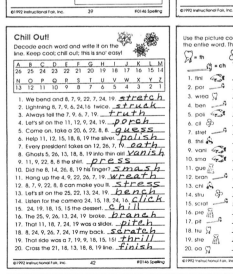

A	B	C	D	E	F	G	H	I	J	K	L	M
26	25	24	23	22	21	20	19	18	17	16	15	14

N	O	P	Q	R	S	T	U	V	W	X	Y	Z
13	12	11	10	9	8	7	6	5	4	3	2	1

1. We bend and 8, 7, 9, 22, 7, 24, 19. stretch
2. Lightning 8, 7, 9, 6, 24, 16 twice. struck
3. Always tell the 7, 9, 6, 7, 19. truth
4. Let's sit on the 11, 12, 9, 24, 19. porch
5. Come on, take a 20, 6, 22, 8, 8. guess
6. Help 11, 12, 15, 18, 8, 19 the silver. polish
7. Every president takes an 12, 26, 7, 19. oath
8. Ghosts 5, 26, 13, 18, 8, 19 into thin air! vanish
9. 11, 9, 22, 8, 8 the shirt. press
10. Did he 8, 14, 26, 8, 19 his finger? smash
11. Hang up the 4, 9, 22, 26, 7, 19. wreath
12. 8, 7, 9, 22, 8, 8 can make you ill. stress
13. Let's sit on the 25, 22, 13, 24, 19. bench
14. Listen for the camera 24, 15, 18, 24, 16. click
15. 24, 19, 18, 15, 15 the dessert. chill
16. The 25, 9, 26, 13, 24, 19 broke. branch
17. That 11, 18, 7, 24, 19 was a slider. pitch
18. 8, 24, 9, 26, 7, 24, 19 my back. scratch
19. That ride was a 7, 19, 9, 18, 15, 15! thrill
20. Cross the 21, 18, 13, 18, 8, 19 line. finish

©1992 Instructional Fair, Inc.   42   IF0146 Spelling

Use the picture code to write each ending. Then write the entire word. The first one has been done for you.

(tooth) = th   (gum/chewing) = ck   (fish) = sh
(bell) = ch   (dress) = ss   (axe) = ll

		finish
1. fini	sh	finish
2. por	ch	porch
3. wrea	th	wreath
4. ben	ch	bench
5. poli	sh	polish
6. cli	ck	click
7. stret	ch	stretch
8. thri	ll	thrill
9. vani	sh	vanish
10. sma	sh	smash
11. gue	ss	guess
12. bran	ch	branch
13. chi	ll	chill
14. stru	ck	struck
15. scrat	ch	scratch
16. pre	ss	press
17. pit	ch	pitch
18. tru	th	truth
19. stre	ss	stress
20. oa	th	oath

©1992 Instructional Fair, Inc.   43   IF0146 Spelling

The Telephone Quiz

"Touch Tone" spelling words are ready for you on "Call Waiting." Decode and write each /f/ and /kw/ word.

Example: 1 = A   8 = W   3 = I

1. 6 - 7 - 3 - 2 - 7 — quiet
2. 6 - 4 - 2 - 6 - 8 - 6 - 1 - 5 - 7 — pheasant
3. 6 - 7 - 3 - 6 - 7 — squirt
4. 5 - 7 - 9 - 6 - 8 - 2 — phrase
5. 7 - 5 - 7 - 3 - 3 — tough
6. 2 - 6 - 7 - 1 - 4 — equal
7. 6 - 7 - 3 - 6 - 5 - 2 — telephone
8. 7 - 6 - 7 - 3 - 6 - 5 — squirm
9. 6 - 7 - 3 - 4 - 7 — quilt
10. 6 - 3 - 5 - 5 - 3 - 1 - 7 — phonics
11. 6 - 6 - 7 - 3 - 6 - 1 - 6 - 3 — photograph
12. 6 - 7 - 2 - 2 - 5 — queen
13. 2 - 5 - 4 - 6 - 3 - 3 - 5 — dolphin
14. 6 - 7 - 3 - 9 — quiz
15. 7 - 6 - 7 - 2 - 2 - 9 - 2 — squeeze
16. 7 - 2 - 5 - 2 - 6 - 3 - 1 - 6 - 3 — telegraph
17. 1 - 5 - 7 - 3 - 3 — cough
18. 7 - 6 - 7 - 1 - 6 - 2 — square
19. 2 - 5 - 2 - 6 - 3 - 1 - 5 - 7 — elephant
20. 6 - 7 - 3 - 1 - 4 - 5 - 2 - 2 — quickly

Use the code to write the name of your city and state.

©1992 Instructional Fair, Inc.   44   IF0146 Spelling

IF0146 Answer Key

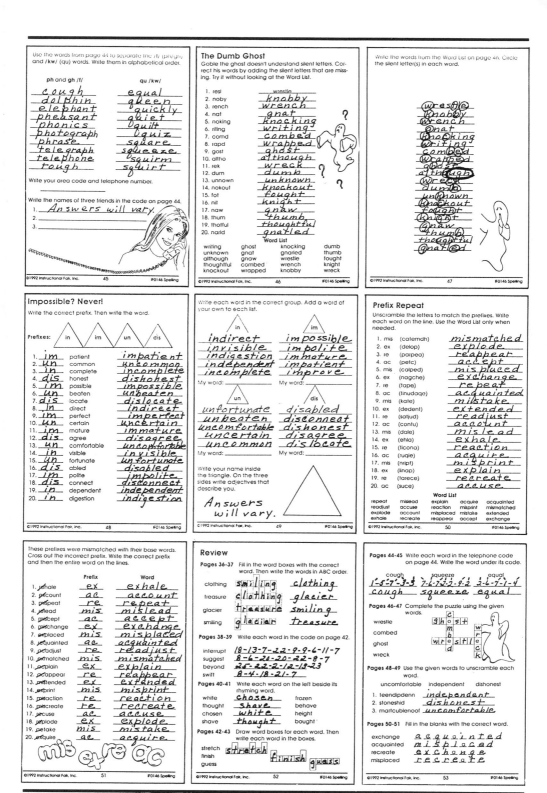

Use the words from page 44 to separate the /f/ (ph/gh) and /kw/ (qu) words. Write them in alphabetical order.

ph and gh /f/
cough
dolphin
elephant
pheasant
phonics
photograph
phrase
telegraph
telephone
tough

qu /kw/
equal
queen
quickly
quiet
quilt
quiz
square
squeeze
squirm
squirt

Write your area code and telephone number.
_____

Write the names of three friends in the code on page 44.
1. Answers will vary.
2. _____
3. _____

The Dumb Ghost

Goble the ghost doesn't understand silent letters. Correct his words by adding the silent letters that are missing. Try it without looking at the Word List.

1. resl — wrestle
2. noby — knobby
3. rench — wrench
4. nat — gnat
5. noking — knocking
6. riting — writing
7. comd — combed
8. rapd — wrapped
9. gost — ghost
10. altho — although
11. rek — wreck
12. dum — dumb
13. unnown — unknown
14. nokout — knockout
15. fot — fought
16. nit — knight
17. naw — gnaw
18. thum — thumb
19. thotful — thoughtful
20. narld — gnarled

Word List

writing	ghost
unknown	gnaw
although	combed
thoughtful	wrapped
knockout	
knocking	dumb
wrestle	thumb
wrench	tought
knobby	knight
wreck	

Write the words from the Word List on page 46. Circle the silent letter(s) in each word.

wrestle
knobby
wrench
gnat
knocking
writing
combed
wrapped
ghost
although
wreck
dumb
unknown
knockout
fought
knight
gnaw
thumb
thoughtful
gnarled

Impossible? Never!

Write the correct prefix. Then write the word.

Prefixes: in   im   un   dis

1. im patient — impatient
2. un common — uncommon
3. in complete — incomplete
4. dis honest — dishonest
5. im possible — impossible
6. un beaten — unbeaten
7. dis locate — dislocate
8. in direct — indirect
9. im perfect — imperfect
10. un certain — uncertain
11. im mature — immature
12. dis agree — disagree
13. un comfortable — uncomfortable
14. in visible — invisible
15. un fortunate — unfortunate
16. dis abled — disabled
17. im polite — impolite
18. dis connect — disconnect
19. in dependent — independent
20. in digestion — indigestion

Write each word in the correct group. Add a word of your own to each list.

in
indirect
invisible
indigestion
independent
incomplete
My word: _____

im
impossible
impolite
immature
impatient
improve
My word: _____

un
unfortunate
unbeaten
uncomfortable
uncertain
uncommon
My word: _____

dis
disabled
disconnect
dishonest
disagree
dislocate
My word: _____

Write your name inside the triangle. On the three sides write adjectives that describe you.

Answers will vary.

Prefix Repeat

Unscramble the letters to match the prefixes. Write each word on the line. Use the Word List only when needed.

1. mis (catemdh) — mismatched
2. ex (delop) — explode
3. re (parpea) — reappear
4. ac (petc) — accept
5. mis (calped) — misplaced
6. ex (nagche) — exchange
7. re (tape) — repeat
8. ac (tinudage) — acquainted
9. mis (kate) — mistake
10. ex (dedent) — extended
11. re (satjud) — readjust
12. ac (contu) — account
13. mis (dale) — mislead
14. ex (ehla) — exhale
15. re (licona) — reaction
16. ac (ruqie) — acquire
17. mis (nript) — misprint
18. ex (linap) — explain
19. re (tarece) — recreate
20. ac (suce) — accuse

Word List

repeat	mislead	explain	acquire	acquainted
readjust	accuse	reaction	misprint	mismatched
explode	account	misplaced	mistake	extended
exhale	recreate	reappear	accept	exchange

These prefixes were mismatched with their base words. Cross out the incorrect prefix. Write the correct prefix and then the entire word on the lines.

	Prefix	Word
1. exhale	ex	exhale
2. account	ac	account
3. repeat	re	repeat
4. mislead	mis	mislead
5. accept	ac	accept
6. exchange	ex	exchange
7. misplaced	mis	misplaced
8. acquainted	ac	acquainted
9. readjust	re	readjust
10. mismatched	mis	mismatched
11. explain	ex	explain
12. reappear	re	reappear
13. extended	ex	extended
14. misprint	mis	misprint
15. reaction	re	reaction
16. recreate	re	recreate
17. accuse	ac	accuse
18. explode	ex	explode
19. mistake	mis	mistake
20. acquire	ac	acquire

mis ex re ac

Review

Pages 36-37 Fill in the word boxes with the correct word. Then write the words in ABC order.

clothing	smiling	clothing
treasure	clothing	glacier
glacier	treasure	smiling
smiling	glacier	treasure

Pages 38-39 Write each word in the code on page 42.

interrupt — 18-13-7-22-9-9-6-11-7
suggest — 8-6-20-20-22-8-7
beyond — 25-2.2-2-12-13-23
swift — 8-4-18-21-7

Pages 40-41 Write each word on the left beside its rhyming word.

white — chosen   frozen
thought — shave   behave
chosen — white   height
shave — thought   bought

Pages 42-43 Draw word boxes for each word. Then write each word in the boxes.

stretch — stretch
finish — finish
guess — guess

Pages 44-45 Write each word in the telephone code on page 44. Write the word under its code.

cough — 1-5-7-3-3
squeeze — 7-7-7-7-9-2
equal — 2-6-7-1-4
cough   squeeze   equal

Pages 46-47 Complete the puzzle using the given words.

wrestle
combed
ghost
wreck

Pages 48-49 Use the given words to unscramble each word.

uncomfortable   independent   dishonest

1. teendidpenn — independent
2. stoneshid — dishonest
3. martcublenoof — uncomfortable

Pages 50-51 Fill in the blanks with the correct word.

exchange	acquainted
acquainted	misplaced
recreate	exchange
misplaced	recreate

Wonderful Winning

Add suffixes to these base words. Write the whole word, dropping and adding letters when necessary.

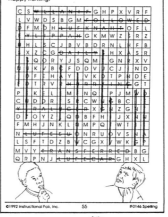

	ed		ing
finish	finished	win	winning
transfer	transferred	hurry	hurrying
discover	discovered	vote	voting
follow	followed	study	studying
paint	painted	share	sharing

	ful		ly
grace	graceful	happy	happily
wonder	wonderful	final	finally
use	useful	day	daily
care	careful	regular	regularly
thank	thankful	sudden	suddenly

1. Which words double a consonant before adding a suffix? tranferred winning
2. Which words drop an e? voting sharing
3. Which words change y to i? happily daily
4. Which words keep the final e of the base word? graceful useful careful
5. Which words keep the final y of the base word? hurrying studying

©1992 Instructional Fair, Inc. 54 IF0146 Spelling

Find the newly formed words from page 54 in this wordsearch. Look across, down and backwards. Happy hunting!

©1992 Instructional Fair, Inc. 55 IF0146 Spelling

Vacation Invitation

Come along on a vacation from the spelling doldrums. Fill in the blanks. Write the boxed letters at the bottom to find out where your surprise vacation will be! Use the Word List at the bottom of page 57.

1. invitation
2. collection
3. occasion
4. imagination
5. addition
6. education
7. conclusion
8. information
9. election
10. concentration
11. subtraction
12. mention
13. division
14. excursion
15. pension
16. multiplication
17. invasion
18. profession
19. mansion
20. vacation

EPCOT CENTER IN FLORIDA

©1992 Instructional Fair, Inc. 56 IF0146 Spelling

Unscramble the first part of each word below. Write the word with its suffix.

1. (dida) tion — addition
2. (curex) sion — excursion
3. (onceratnc) tion — concentration
4. (nep) sion — pension
5. (sofepr) sion — profession
6. (mainrof) tion — information
7. (coca) sion — occasion
8. (ratbusc) tion — subtraction
9. (cava) tion — vacation
10. (ucclon) sion — conclusion
11. (vidi) sion — division
12. (agiminan) tion — imagination
13. (amn) sion — mansion
14. (clocel) tion — collection
15. (vain) sion — invasion
16. (lumpticaii) tion — multiplication
17. (cele) tion — election
18. (nem) tion — mention
19. (acude) tion — education
20. (tanivi) tion — invitation

Word List

profession	concentration	invitation	addition
excursion	multiplication	occasion	invasion
information	imagination	mansion	pension
education	subtraction	mention	election
collection	conclusion	vacation	division

©1992 Instructional Fair, Inc. 57 IF0146 Spelling

Let's Go!

We're off to the Contraction "20" Speedway. Write the contraction next to each word group. Then write the letters that were removed to form the contraction.

1. they had — they'd — ha
2. it will — it'll — wi
3. were not — weren't — o
4. who is — who's — i
5. will not — won't — ill o
6. does not — doesn't — o
7. let us — let's — u
8. what is — what's — i
9. I would — I'd — would
10. should have — should've — ha
11. where is — where's — i
12. you will — you'll — wi
13. we have — we've — ha
14. had not — hadn't — o
15. here is — here's — i
16. we will — we'll — wi
17. are not — aren't — o
18. we are — we're — a
19. there is — there's — i
20. would not — wouldn't — o

Word List

here's	doesn't	wouldn't	I'd
we're	aren't	should've	it'll
weren't	they'd	we've	let's
where's	there's	hadn't	we'll
you'll	what's	won't	who's

©1992 Instructional Fair, Inc. 58 IF0146 Spelling

Write the two words which formed each contraction.

1. let's — let — us
2. we're — we — are
3. weren't — were — not
4. where's — where — is
5. you'll — you — will
6. wouldn't — would — not
7. doesn't — does — not
8. aren't — are — not
9. they'd — they — had
10. there's — there — is
11. what's — what — is
12. should've — should — have
13. we've — we — have
14. it'll — it — will
15. I'd — I — would
16. hadn't — had — not
17. who's — who — is
18. here's — here — is
19. we'll — we — will
20. won't — will — not

©1992 Instructional Fair, Inc. 59 IF0146 Spelling

"Y's" About Plurals

Change y to i and add es to make these words plural. Then number the words in alphabetical order. "Owl" bet you can do it easily!

1. battery — batteries — 2
2. country — countries — 9
3. enemy — enemies — 10
4. company — companies — 7
5. mystery — mysteries — 15
6. cavity — cavities — 4
7. copy — copies — 8
8. secretary — secretaries — 16
9. trophy — trophies — 20
10. family — families — 11
11. story — stories — 17
12. library — libraries — 14
13. grocery — groceries — 12
14. strawberry — strawberries — 18
15. city — cities — 6
16. study — studies — 19
17. army — armies — 1
18. butterfly — butterflies — 3
19. cherry — cherries — 5
20. guppy — guppies — 13

Challenge: After numbering in ABC order, which words would these math equations represent?

7 + 6 = companies + cities = guppies
8 + 9 = copies + countries = stories
5 + 11 = cherries + families = secretaries

©1992 Instructional Fair, Inc. 60 IF0146 Spelling

Write the words that would fit into these box puzzles. Use the plurals from the previous page.

1. trophies
2. studies
3. companies
4. copies
5. strawberries
6. guppies
7. stories
8. butterflies
9. batteries
10. groceries
11. cities
12. mysteries
13. armies
14. families
15. libraries
16. countries
17. cherries
18. cavities
19. secretaries
20. enemies

Write your full name in a box puzzle. **Hint:** Remember to give capital letters a tall box.

©1992 Instructional Fair, Inc. 61 IF0146 Spelling

Videos

"Fast forward" to the code box to decode these plurals. Then "eject" the plural and write the base word.

1. qcoqvsg — COUCHES — COUCH
2. holwg — TAXIS — TAXI
3. psoqvsg — BEACHES — BEACH
4. gdzwbhg — SPLINTS — SPLINT
5. kwhqvsg — WITCHES — WITCH
6. hfoqvg — TRACKS — TRACK
7. cghfwqvsg — OSTRICHES — OSTRICH
8. dofsbhg — PARENTS — PARENT
9. smszogvsg — EYELASHES — EYELASH
10. qzoggsg — CLASSES — CLASS
11. jwrscg — VIDEOS — VIDEO
12. poffszg — BARRELS — BARREL
13. fcrscg — RODEOS — RODEO
14. aohqvsg — MATCHES — MATCH
15. dwzzckg — PILLOWS — PILLOW
16. pfigvsg — BRUSHES — BRUSH
17. gvihhzsg — SHUTTLES — SHUTTLE
18. pfobqvsg — BRANCHES — BRANCH
19. uwfzg — GIRLS — GIRL
20. pigsg — BUSES — BUS

Code Box	A	B	C	D	E	F	G	H	I	J	K	L
	o	p	q	r	s	t	u	v	w	x	y	z
	M	N	O	P	Q	R	S	T	U	V	W	X	Y	Z
	a	b	c	d	e	f	g	h	i	j	k	l	m	n

©1992 Instructional Fair, Inc. 62 IF0146 Spelling

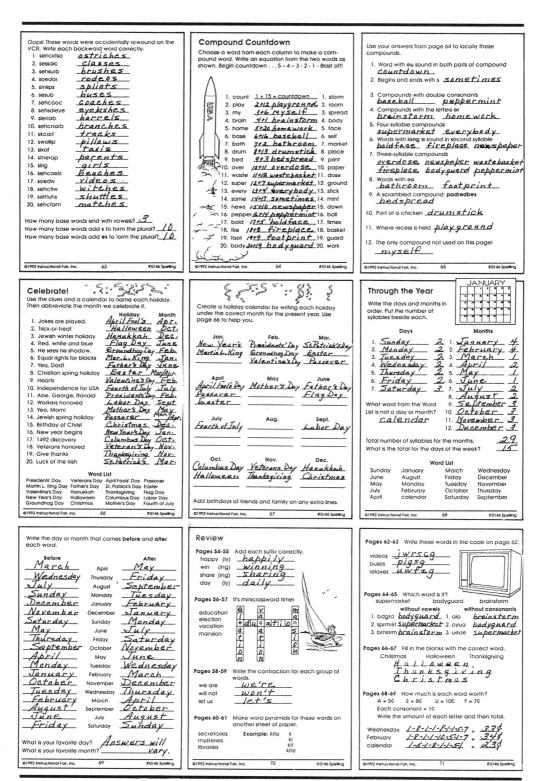

Panel 1 (page 63):

Oops! These words were accidentally rewound on the VCR. Write each backward word correctly.

1. sehcirtso — ostriches
2. sessalc — classes
3. sehsurb — brushes
4. soedor — rodeos
5. stnilps — splints
6. sesub — buses
7. sehcaoc — coaches
8. sehsaleye — eyelashes
9. slerrab — barrels
10. sehcnarb — branches
11. skcart — tracks
12. swollip — pillows
13. sixat — taxis
14. stnerap — parents
15. slrig — girls
16. sehcaeb — beaches
17. soediv — videos
18. sehctiw — witches
19. selttuhs — shuttles
20. sehctam — matches

How many base words end with vowels? 3
How many base words add s to form the plural? 10
How many base words add es to form the plural? 10

©1992 Instructional Fair, Inc. 63 IF0146 Spelling

Panel 2 (page 64): Compound Countdown

Choose a word from each column to make a compound word. Write an equation from the two words as shown. Begin countdown . . . 5 - 4 - 3 - 2 - 1 - Blast off!

1. count — 1 + 15 = countdown — 1. storm
2. play — 2+12 playground — 2. room
3. my — 3+6 myself — 3. spread
4. brain — 4+1 brainstorm — 4. body
5. home — 5+20 homework — 5. face
6. base — 6+6 baseball — 6. self
7. bath — 7+2 bathroom — 7. market
8. drum — 8+13 drumstick — 8. place
9. bed — 9+3 bedspread — 9. print
10. over — 10+1 overdose — 10. paper
11. waste — 11+18 wastebasket — 11. dose
12. super — 12+7 supermarket — 12. ground
13. every — 13+4 everybody — 13. stick
14. some — 14+17 sometimes — 14. mint
15. news — 15+10 newspaper — 15. down
16. pepper — 16+14 peppermint — 16. ball
17. bold — 17+5 boldface — 17. times
18. fire — 18+8 fireplace — 18. basket
19. foot — 19+9 footprint — 19. guard
20. body — 20+19 bodyguard — 20. work

©1992 Instructional Fair, Inc. 64 IF0146 Spelling

Panel 3 (page 65):

Use your answers from page 64 to locate these compounds.

1. Word with ou sound in both parts of compound — countdown
2. Begins and ends with s — sometimes
3. Compounds with double consonants — baseball peppermint
4. Compounds with the letters er — brainstorm homework
5. Four-syllable compounds — supermarket everybody
6. Words with long o sound in second syllable — boldface fireplace newspaper
7. Three-syllable compounds — overdose newspaper wastebasket fireplace bodyguard peppermint
8. Words with oo — bathroom footprint
9. A scrambled compound: padredbes — bedspread
10. Part of a chicken — drumstick
11. Where recess is held — playground
12. The only compound not used on this page! — myself

©1992 Instructional Fair, Inc. 65 IF0146 Spelling

Panel 4 (page 66): Celebrate!

Use the clues and a calendar to name each holiday. Then abbreviate the month we celebrate it.

	Holiday	Month
1. Jokes are played.	April Fool's	Apr.
2. Trick-or-treat	Halloween	Oct.
3. Jewish winter holiday	Hanukkah	Dec.
4. Red, white and blue	Flag Day	June
5. He sees his shadow.	Groundhog Day	Feb.
6. Equal rights for blacks	Mar. L. King	Jan.
7. Yea, Dad!	Father's Day	June
8. Christian spring holiday	Easter	Mar./Apr.
9. Hearts	Valentine's Day	Feb.
10. Independence for USA	Fourth of July	July
11. Abe, George, Ronald	Presidents' Day	Feb.
12. Workers honored	Labor Day	Sept.
13. Yea, Mom!	Mother's Day	May
14. Jewish spring holiday	Passover	Mar./Apr.
15. Birthday of Christ	Christmas	Dec.
16. New year begins	New Year's Day	Jan.
17. 1492 discovery	Columbus Day	Oct.
18. Veterans honored	Veteran's Day	Nov.
19. Give thanks	Thanksgiving	Nov.
20. Luck of the Irish	St. Patrick's	Mar.

Word List
Presidents' Day Veterans Day April Fools' Day Passover
Martin L. King Day Father's Day St. Patrick's Day Easter
Valentine's Day Hanukkah Thanksgiving Flag Day
New Year's Day Halloween Columbus Day Labor Day
Groundhog Day Christmas Mother's Day Fourth of July

©1992 Instructional Fair, Inc. 66 IF0146 Spelling

Panel 5 (page 67):

Create a holiday calendar by writing each holiday under the correct month for the present year. Use page 66 to help you.

Jan.	Feb.	Mar.
New Year's	Presidents' Day	St. Patrick's Day
Martin L. King	Groundhog Day	Easter
	Valentine's Day	Passover

April	May	June
April Fool's Day	Mother's Day	Father's Day
Passover		Flag Day
Easter		

July	Aug.	Sept.
Fourth of July		Labor Day

Oct.	Nov.	Dec.
Columbus Day	Veterans Day	Hanukkah
Halloween	Thanksgiving	Christmas

Add birthdays of friends and family on any extra lines.

©1992 Instructional Fair, Inc. 67 IF0146 Spelling

Panel 6 (page 68): Through the Year

JANUARY

Write the days and months in order. Put the number of syllables beside each.

Days
1. Sunday — 2
2. Monday — 2
3. Tuesday — 2
4. Wednesday — 2
5. Thursday — 2
6. Friday — 2
7. Saturday — 3

Months
1. January — 4
2. February — 4
3. March — 1
4. April — 2
5. May — 1
6. June — 1
7. July — 2
8. August — 2
9. September — 3
10. October — 3
11. November — 3
12. December — 3

What word from the Word List is not a day or month? calendar

Total number of syllables for the months. 29
What is the total for the days of the week? 15

Word List
Sunday January March Wednesday
June August Friday December
May Monday Tuesday November
July February October Thursday
April calendar Saturday September

©1992 Instructional Fair, Inc. 68 IF0146 Spelling

Panel 7 (page 69):

Write the day or month that comes before and after each word.

Before		After
March	April	May
Wednesday	Thursday	Friday
July	August	September
Sunday	Monday	Tuesday
December	January	February
November	December	January
Saturday	Sunday	Monday
May	June	July
Thursday	Friday	Saturday
September	October	November
April	May	June
Monday	Tuesday	Wednesday
January	February	March
October	November	December
Tuesday	Wednesday	Thursday
February	March	April
August	September	October
June	July	August
Friday	Saturday	Sunday

What is your favorite day? Answers will
What is your favorite month? vary.

©1992 Instructional Fair, Inc. 69 IF0146 Spelling

Panel 8 (page 70): Review

Pages 54-55 Add each suffix correctly.
happy (ly) — happily
win (ing) — winning
share (ing) — sharing
day (ly) — daily

Pages 56-57 It's minicrossword time!

education
election
vacation
mansion

(crossword: e d u c a t i o n, with vowels/election/vacation/mansion intersecting)

Pages 58-59 Write the contraction for each group of words.
we are — we're
will not — won't
let us — let's

Pages 60-61 Make word pyramids for these words on another sheet of paper.
secretaries
mysteries
libraries

Example: kite
k
ki
kit
kite

©1992 Instructional Fair, Inc. 70 IF0146 Spelling

Panel 9 (page 71):

Pages 62-63 Write these words in the code on page 62.
videos — jwrscg
buses — pigsg
relaxes — uwfzg

Pages 64-65 Which word is it?
supermarket bodyguard brainstorm

without vowels
1. bdgrd — bodyguard
2. sprmkt — supermarket
3. brnstrm — brainstorm

without consonants
1. aio — brainstorm
2. oyua — bodyguard
3. ueae — supermarket

Pages 66-67 Fill in the blanks with the correct word.
Christmas Halloween Thanksgiving
Halloween.
Thanksgiving.
Christmas.

Pages 68-69 How much is each word worth?
A = 5¢ E = 8¢ U = 10¢ Y = 7¢
Each consonant = 1¢
Write the amount of each letter and then total.

Wednesday — 1-8-1-1-8-1-1-5-7 = 33¢
February — 1-8-1-1-10-5-1-7 = 34¢
calendar — 1-5-1-8-1-1-5-1 = 23¢

©1992 Instructional Fair, Inc. 71 IF0146 Spelling

©1992 Instructional Fair, Inc. IF0146 Answer Key

Circle the misspelled word in each sentence. Write it correctly on the line. Don't "sneak" a peek at the previous page!

1. Mercury is closser to the Sun than Earth. _____
2. Flaims were shooting out of the plane. _____
3. We studied about glasiers in geography. _____
4. Mom was smileing because she was proud of me. _____
5. There is a skeleten in the closet. _____
6. The leaves are swirlling in the wind. _____
7. Jeff inherited a trate from our mother. _____
8. Water and wind make sharp rocks smothe. _____
9. John is a very skeptacal person. _____
10. Choose a prize from the treashur chest! _____
11. A glob has lines of latitude and longitude. _____
12. Give used clotheing to the needy. _____
13. Mary gave a swif answer. _____
14. I got caught in a traffic snarle. _____
15. Our butcher uses a cleavver. _____
16. He needed help climming the tree. _____
17. We have a skatebroad park in our town. _____
18. This sweatar is itchy. _____
19. Mom brought home glased donuts. _____
20. Put flowr on the grocery list. _____

Stamp Command

Unscramble the letters and write the word. Then circle the final consonant blend. You can "lick" these words!

29

1. tatpetm _____
2. pectex· _____
3. nobyed _____
4. eldish _____
5. gutsges _____
6. momcadn _____
7. pastm _____
8. tansint _____
9. purtinret _____
10. twfis _____
11. lyeid _____
12. ectollc _____
13. ansitdt _____
14. drefin _____
15. countdc _____
16. rismhp _____
17. recrunt _____
18. drimen _____
19. stoneh _____
20. enomtm _____

Word List

shield
collect
swift
attempt
conduct
interrupt
honest
suggest
distant
remind
expect
current
command
moment
beyond
shrimp
instant
friend
stamp
yield

Design three new stamps.

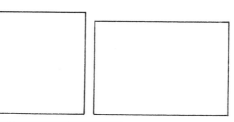

Fill in the final consonant blends. Then rewrite the list in alphabetical order.

1. swi __ __ _____
2. dista __ __ _____
3. comma __ __ _____
4. frie __ __ _____
5. shie __ __ _____
6. hone __ __ _____
7. expe __ __ _____
8. beyo __ __ _____
9. condu __ __ _____
10. colle __ __ _____
11. curre __ __ _____
12. insta __ __ _____
13. attem __ __ _____
14. remi __ __ _____
15. mome __ __ _____
16. interru __ __ _____
17. shri __ __ _____
18. yie __ __ _____
19. sugge __ __ _____
20. sta __ __ _____

Stamp Out _____ !

Stand up for a cause. Design a poster to help save our Earth.

Which Whale?

Add one of these consonant digraphs to each group of letters to make a word. Which whale should you choose? Write the word.

th   wh   sh   ch

1. _____ ade _____
2. _____ ich _____
3. _____ eated _____
4. _____ adow _____
5. _____ eir _____
6. _____ immer _____
7. _____ ile _____
8. _____ ought _____
9. _____ eel _____
10. _____ ough _____
11. _____ ave _____
12. _____ aw _____
13. _____ osen _____
14. _____ irsty _____
15. _____ ildren _____
16. _____ ite _____
17. _____ outed _____
18. _____ orus _____
19. _____ ale _____
20. _____ airman _____

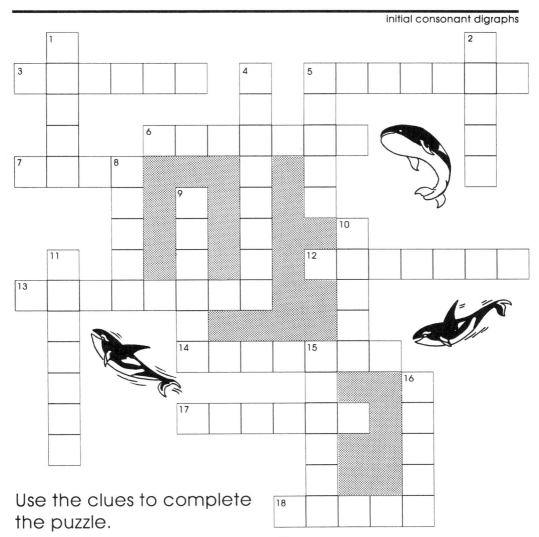

Use the clues to complete the puzzle.

Across

3. picked or selected
5. past tense of think
6. was dishonest
7. opposite of freeze
12. rhymes with glimmer
13. young boys and girls
14. yelled
17. shaded area when light is blocked
18. out of the sun

Down

1. sounds like witch
2. rhymes with file
4. head person
5. homophone of they're and there
8. a tire
9. group of singers
10. large ocean mammal
11. wanting to drink
15. rhymes with dough
16. remove facial hair

Chill Out!

Decode each word and write it on the line. Keep cool; chill out; this is sno' easy!

A	B	C	D	E	F	G	H	I	J	K	L	M
26	25	24	23	22	21	20	19	18	17	16	15	14

N	O	P	Q	R	S	T	U	V	W	X	Y	Z
13	12	11	10	9	8	7	6	5	4	3	2	1

1. We bend and 8, 7, 9, 22, 7, 24, 19. _____

2. Lightning 8, 7, 9, 6, 24,16 twice. _____

3. Always tell the 7, 9, 6, 7, 19. _____

4. Let's sit on the 11, 12, 9, 24, 19. _____

5. Come on, take a 20, 6, 22, 8, 8. _____

6. Help 11, 12, 15, 18, 8, 19 the silver. _____

7. Every president takes an 12, 26, 7, 19. _____

8. Ghosts 5, 26, 13, 18, 8, 19 into thin air! _____

9. 11, 9, 22, 8, 8 the shirt. _____

10. Did he 8, 14, 26, 8, 19 his finger? _____

11. Hang up the 4, 9, 22, 26, 7, 19. _____

12. 8, 7, 9, 22, 8, 8 can make you ill. _____

13. Let's sit on the 25, 22, 13, 24, 19. _____

14. Listen for the camera 24, 15, 18, 24, 16. _____

15. 24, 19, 18, 15, 15 the dessert. _____

16. The 25, 9, 26, 13, 24, 19 broke. _____

17. That 11, 18, 7, 24, 19 was a slider. _____

18. 8, 24, 9, 26, 7, 24, 19 my back. _____

19. That ride was a 7, 19, 9, 18, 15, 15! _____

20. Cross the 21, 18, 13, 18, 8, 19 line. _____

Use the picture code to write each ending. Then write the entire word. The first one has been done for you.

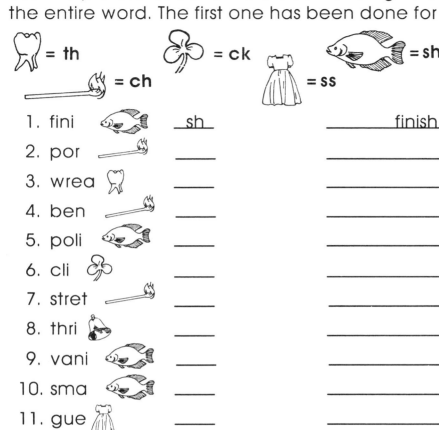

= th   = ck   = sh   = ss   = ch   = ll

1. fini 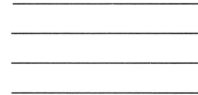 __sh__ __finish__

2. por __ __

3. wrea __ __

4. ben __ __

5. poli __ __

6. cli __ __

7. stret __ __

8. thri __ __

9. vani __ __

10. sma __ __

11. gue __ __

12. bran __ __

13. chi __ __

14. stru __ __

15. scrat __ __

16. pre __ __

17. pit __ __

18. tru  __ __

19. stre __ __

20. oa 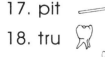 __ __

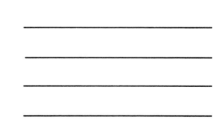

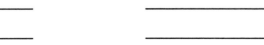

The Telephone Quiz

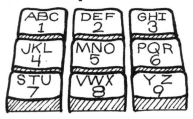

"Touch Tone" spelling words are ready for you on "Call Waiting." Decode and write each /**f**/ and /**kw**/ word.

Example: 1 = A   8 = W   3 = I

1. 6 – 7 – 3 – 2 – 7 _____

2. 6 – 3 – 2 – 1 – 7 – 1 – 5 – 7 _____

3. 7 – 6 – 7 – 3 – 6 – 7 _____

4. 6 – 3 – 6 – 1 – 7 – 2 _____

5. 7 – 5 – 7 – 3 – 3 _____

6. 2 – 6 – 7 – 1 – 4 _____

7. 7 – 2 – 4 – 2 – 6 – 3 – 5 – 5 – 2 _____

8. 7 – 6 – 7 – 3 – 6 – 5 _____

9. 6 – 7 – 3 – 4 – 7 _____

10. 6 – 3 – 5 – 5 – 3 – 1 – 7 _____

11. 6 – 3 – 5 – 7 – 5 – 3 – 6 – 1 – 6 – 3 _____

12. 6 – 7 – 2 – 2 – 5 _____

13. 2 – 5 – 4 – 6 – 3 – 3 – 5 _____

14. 6 – 7 – 3 – 9 _____

15. 7 – 6 – 7 – 2 – 2 – 9 – 2 _____

16. 7 – 2 – 4 – 2 – 3 – 6 – 1 – 6 – 3 _____

17. 1 – 5 – 7 – 3 – 3 _____

18. 7 – 6 – 7 – 1 – 6 – 2 _____

19. 2 – 4 – 2 – 6 – 3 – 1 – 5 – 7 _____

20. 6 – 7 – 3 – 1 – 4 – 4 – 9 _____

Use the code to write the name of your city and state.

_____   _____

Use the words from page 44 to separate the /**f**/ (ph/gh) and /**kw**/ (qu) words. Write them in alphabetical order.

ph and **gh** /**f**/   **qu** /**kw**/

_____   _____

_____   _____

_____   _____

_____   _____

_____   _____

_____   _____

_____   _____

_____   _____

_____   _____

_____

Write your area code and telephone number.

_____

Write the names of three friends in the code on page 44.

1. _____

2. _____

3. _____

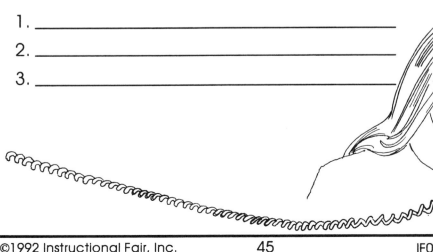

The Dumb Ghost

Goble the ghost doesn't understand silent letters. Correct his words by adding the silent letters that are missing. Try it without looking at the Word List.

1. resl   _____wrestle_____
2. noby   _____
3. rench   _____
4. nat   _____
5. noking   _____
6. riting   _____
7. comd   _____
8. rapd   _____
9. gost   _____
10. altho   _____
11. rek   _____
12. dum   _____
13. unnown   _____
14. nokout   _____
15. fot   _____
16. nit   _____
17. naw   _____
18. thum   _____
19. thotful   _____
20. narld   _____

Word List

writing	ghost	knocking	dumb
unknown	gnat	gnarled	thumb
although	gnaw	wrestle	fought
thoughtful	combed	wrench	knight
knockout	wrapped	knobby	wreck

Write the words from the Word List on page 46. Circle the silent letter(s) in each word.

Impossible? Never!

Write the correct prefix. Then write the word.

Prefixes: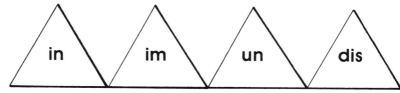

1. _____ patient   _____
2. _____ common   _____
3. _____ complete   _____
4. _____ honest   _____
5. _____ possible   _____
6. _____ beaten   _____
7. _____ locate   _____
8. _____ direct   _____
9. _____ perfect   _____
10. _____ certain   _____
11. _____ mature   _____
12. _____ agree   _____
13. _____ comfortable   _____
14. _____ visible   _____
15. _____ fortunate   _____
16. _____ abled   _____
17. _____ polite   _____
18. _____ connect   _____
19. _____ dependent   _____
20. _____ digestion   _____

Write each word in the correct group. Add a word of your own to each list.

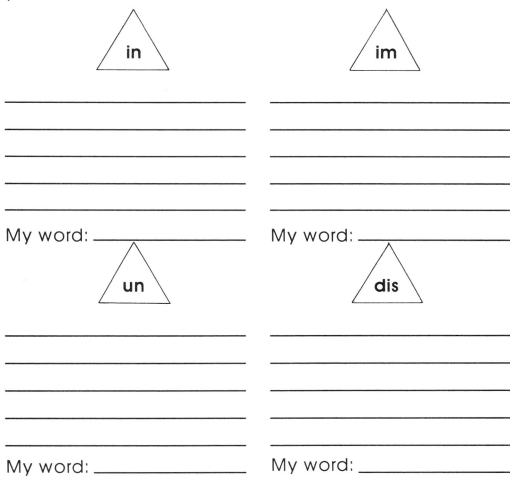

in

_____
_____
_____
_____
_____

My word: _____

im

_____
_____
_____
_____
_____

My word: _____

un

_____
_____
_____
_____

My word: _____

dis

_____
_____
_____
_____

My word: _____

Write your name inside the triangle. On the three sides write adjectives that describe you.

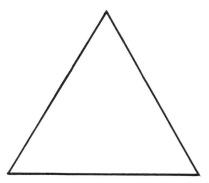

Prefix Repeat

Unscramble the letters to match the prefixes. Write each word on the line. Use the Word List only when needed.

1. mis   (catemdh)   _____
2. ex   (delop)   _____
3. re   (parpea)   _____
4. ac   (petc)   _____
5. mis   (calped)   _____
6. ex   (nagche)   _____
7. re   (tape)   _____
8. ac   (tinudaqe) _____
9. mis   (kate)   _____
10. ex   (dedent)   _____
11. re   (satjud)   _____
12. ac   (contu)   _____
13. mis (dale)   _____
14. ex   (ehla)   _____
15. re   (ticona)   _____
16. ac   (ruqie)   _____
17. mis (nript)   _____
18. ex   (linap)   _____
19. re   (tarece)   _____
20. ac   (suce)   _____

Word List

repeat	mislead	explain	acquire	acquainted
readjust	accuse	reaction	misprint	mismatched
explode	account	misplaced	mistake	extended
exhale	recreate	reappear	accept	exchange

These prefixes were mismatched with their base words. Cross out the incorrect prefix. Write the correct prefix and then the entire word on the lines.

	Prefix	**Word**
1. rehale	_____	_____
2. excount	_____	_____
3. mispeat	_____	_____
4. relead	_____	_____
5. miscept	_____	_____
6. mischange	_____	_____
7. explaced	_____	_____
8. requainted	_____	_____
9. acadjust	_____	_____
10. exmatched	_____	_____
11. acplain	_____	_____
12. acappear	_____	_____
13. mistended	_____	_____
14. exprint	_____	_____
15. misaction	_____	_____
16. miscreate	_____	_____
17. recuse	_____	_____
18. replode	_____	_____
19. actake	_____	_____
20. exquire	_____	_____

mis ex re ac

Review

Pages 36-37 Fill in the word boxes with the correct word. Then write the words in ABC order.

clothing

treasure

glacier

smiling

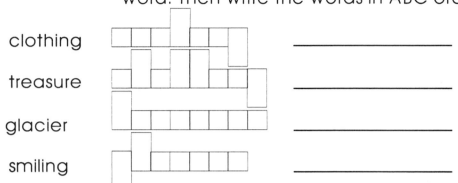

_____

_____

_____

_____

Pages 38-39 Write each word in the code on page 42.

interrupt _____

suggest _____

beyond _____

swift _____

Pages 40-41 Write each word on the left beside its rhyming word.

white _____ frozen

thought _____ behave

chosen _____ height

shave _____ bought

Pages 42-43 Draw word boxes for each word. Then write each word in the boxes.

stretch

finish

guess

Pages 44-45 Write each word in the telephone code on page 44. Write the word under its code.

cough   squeeze   equal

_____   _____   _____

_____   _____   _____

Pages 46-47 Complete the puzzle using the given words.

wrestle

combed

ghost

wreck

Pages 48-49 Use the given words to unscramble each word.

uncomfortable   independent   dishonest

1. teendipdenn   _____
2. stoneshid   _____
3. martcublenoof _____

Pages 50-51 Fill in the blanks with the correct word.

exchange   __ __ __ __ a __ __ __ __
acquainted   __ __ __ __ __ a __ __ __
recreate   __ __ __ __ a __ __ __
misplaced   __ __ __ __ __ a __ __

Wonderful Winning

Add suffixes to these base words. Write the whole word, dropping and adding letters when necessary.

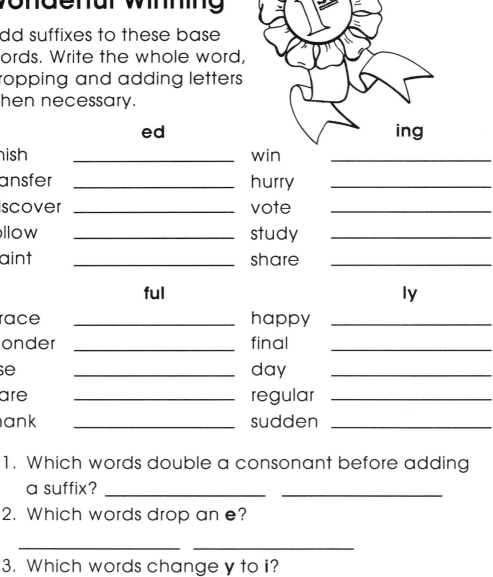

ed			**ing**	
finish	_____	win	_____
transfer	_____	hurry	_____
discover	_____	vote	_____
follow	_____	study	_____
paint	_____	share	_____

ful			**ly**	
grace	_____	happy	_____
wonder	_____	final	_____
use	_____	day	_____
care	_____	regular	_____
thank	_____	sudden	_____

1. Which words double a consonant before adding a suffix? _____ _____

2. Which words drop an **e**?
   _____ _____

3. Which words change **y** to **i**?
   _____ _____

4. Which words keep the final **e** of the base word?
   _____ _____ _____

5. Which words keep the final **y** of the base word?
   _____ _____

Find the newly formed words from page 54 in this wordsearch. Look across, down and backwards. Happy hunting!

C	S	Y	L	L	A	N	I	F	G	H	P	X	V	R	F
L	V	W	D	S	B	G	M	F	O	L	L	O	W	E	D
D	F	M	D	H	L	U	F	K	N	A	H	T	O	F	L
E	Y	L	I	P	P	A	H	G	K	M	W	Z	S	R	Z
H	H	L	S	C	J	B	V	B	D	R	N	L	H	F	B
S	X	Z	C	G	D	A	I	L	Y	S	H	X	A	S	R
I	S	Q	O	R	Y	J	S	Q	M	T	G	N	R	X	V
N	U	K	V	B	C	F	D	D	V	U	C	J	I	N	D
I	D	F	E	H	A	Y	L	V	K	D	T	P	N	D	E
F	D	T	R	V	R	H	U	R	R	Y	I	N	G	G	T
P	E	K	E	L	E	M	F	N	Q	I	P	J	M	W	D
C	N	D	D	R	F	S	R	C	W	N	G	B	C	I	E
Y	L	R	A	L	U	G	E	R	X	G	N	Z	G	N	T
D	Y	O	Y	Z	L	Q	D	B	F	H	I	J	X	N	N
F	M	H	J	N	K	L	N	M	P	Q	T	W	T	I	I
N	L	U	F	E	S	U	O	N	R	U	O	V	S	N	A
L	S	F	T	D	Z	B	W	C	G	X	V	W	K	G	P
M	V	Y	T	R	A	N	S	F	E	R	R	E	D	B	G
Q	R	P	N	J	L	U	F	E	C	A	R	G	H	X	L

Vacation Invitation

Come along on a vacation from the spelling doldrums.
Fill in the blanks. Write the boxed letters at the bottom to
find out where your surprise vacation will be! Use the
Word List at the bottom of page 57.

1. __ __ V ☐ __ __ __ __ __ __
2. ☐ __ L L __ __ __ __ __ __
3. O __ __ __ __ ☐ __
4. __ M __ __ ☐ __ __ __
5. A __ __ __ __ __ __ ☐
6. __ ☐ U __ __ __ __ __
7. __ ☐ __ C __ U __ __ __ __
8. __ __ F __ ☐ __ __ __ __
9. __ L ☐ __ __ __ __
10. __ __ __ C __ __ ☐ __ __ __
11. __ __ B __ __ __ __ __ __ __
12. __ ☐ __ T __ __ __
13. __ __ V __ __ __ ☐
14. __ X ☐ __ __ __ __ __
15. P ☐ __ __ __ __
16. M __ ☐ __ __ __ __ ☐ __ __ __
17. __ N __ ☐ __ __ __ __
18. ☐ __ __ ☐ __ S S __ __ __
19. M __ __ S __ __ __
20. V __ C __ ☐ __ __ __

__ __ __ __ __   __ __ __ __ __ __
12 18a 2 7 16b   14 9 5 20 15 8

__ __   __ __ __ __ __ __ __ __
4 13   18b 16a 3 10 1 6 17

Unscramble the first part of each word below. Write the word with its suffix.

1. (dida) tion _____
2. (curex) sion _____
3. (onceratnc) tion _____
4. (nep) sion _____
5. (sofepr) sion _____
6. (mainrof) tion _____
7. (coca) sion _____
8. (ratbusc) tion _____
9. (cava) tion _____
10. (ucclon) sion _____
11. (vidi) sion _____
12. (agimian) tion _____
13. (amn) sion _____
14. (clocel) tion _____
15. (vain) sion _____
16. (lumpticail) tion _____
17. (cele) tion _____
18. (nem) tion _____
19. (acude) tion _____
20. (tanivi) tion _____

Word List

profession	concentration	invitation	addition
excursion	multiplication	occasion	invasion
information	imagination	mansion	pension
education	subtraction	mention	election
collection	conclusion	vacation	division

Let's Go!

We're off to the Contraction "20" Speedway. Write the contraction next to each word group. Then write the letters that were removed to form the contraction.

1. they had _____ _____
2. it will _____ _____
3. were not _____ _____
4. who is _____ _____
5. will not _____ _____
6. does not _____ _____
7. let us _____ _____
8. what is _____ _____
9. I would _____ _____
10. should have _____ _____
11. where is _____ _____
12. you will _____ _____
13. we have _____ _____
14. had not _____ _____
15. here is _____ _____
16. we will _____ _____
17. are not _____ _____
18. we are _____ _____
19. there is _____ _____
20. would not _____ _____

Word List

here's	doesn't	wouldn't	I'd
we're	aren't	should've	it'll
weren't	they'd	we've	let's
where's	there's	hadn't	we'll
you'll	what's	won't	who's

Write the two words which formed each contraction.

1. let's   _____   _____

2. we're   _____   _____

3. weren't   _____   _____

4. where's   _____   _____

5. you'll   _____   _____

6. wouldn't   _____   _____

7. doesn't   _____   _____

8. aren't   _____   _____

9. they'd   _____   _____

10. there's   _____   _____

11. what's   _____   _____

12. should've   _____   _____

13. we've   _____   _____

14. it'll   _____   _____

15. I'd   _____   _____

16. hadn't   _____   _____

17. who's   _____   _____

18. here's   _____   _____

19. we'll   _____   _____

20. won't   _____   _____

"Y's" About Plurals

Change **y** to **i** and add **es** to make these words plural. Then number the words in alphabetical order. "Owl" bet you can do it easily!

1. battery _____ _____
2. country _____ _____
3. enemy _____ _____
4. company _____ _____
5. mystery _____ _____
6. cavity _____ _____
7. copy _____ _____
8. secretary _____ _____
9. trophy _____ _____
10. family _____ _____
11. story _____ _____
12. library _____ _____
13. grocery _____ _____
14. strawberry _____ _____
15. city _____ _____
16. study _____ _____
17. army _____ _____
18. butterfly _____ _____
19. cherry _____ _____
20. guppy _____ _____

Challenge: After numbering in ABC order, which words would these math equations represent?

$7 + 6$ = _____ + _____ = _____
$8 + 9$ = _____ + _____ = _____
$5 + 11$ = _____ + _____ = _____

Write the words that would fit into these box puzzles.
Use the plurals from the previous page.

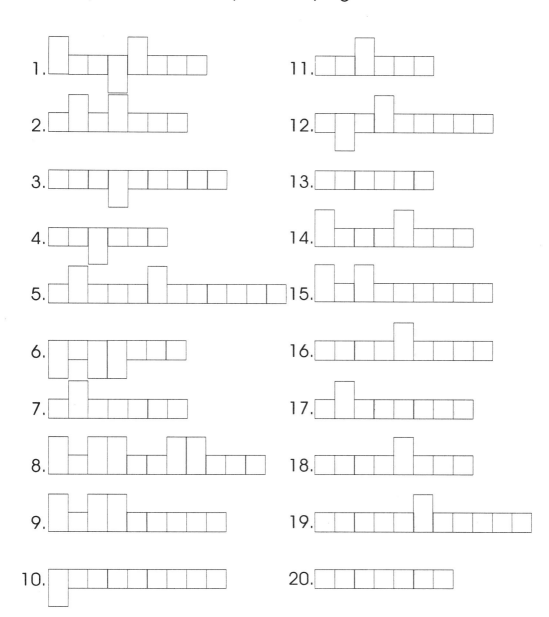

1.
2.
3.
4.
5.
6.
7.
8.
9.
10.
11.
12.
13.
14.
15.
16.
17.
18.
19.
20.

Write your full name in a box puzzle. **Hint:** Remember to give capital letters a tall box.

Videos

"Fast forward" to the code box to write these plurals.
Then "eject" the plural and write the base word.

1. qcoqvsg _____ _____
2. holwg _____ _____
3. psoqvsg _____ _____
4. gdzwbhg _____ _____
5. kwhqvsg _____ _____
6. hfoqyg _____ _____
7. cghfwqvsg _____ _____
8. dofsbhg _____ _____
9. smszogvsg _____ _____
10. qzoggsg _____ _____
11. jwrscg _____ _____
12. poffszg _____ _____
13. fcrscg _____ _____
14. aohqvsg _____ _____
15. dwzzckg _____ _____
16. pfigvsg _____ _____
17. gvihhzsg _____ _____
18. pfobqvsg _____ _____
19. uwfzg _____ _____
20. pigsg _____ _____

Code Box	A	B	C	D	E	F	G	H	I	J	K	L
	o	p	q	r	s	t	u	v	w	x	y	z
	M	N	O	P	Q	R	S	T	U	V	W	X	Y	Z
	a	b	c	d	e	f	g	h	i	j	k	l	m	n

Oops! These words were accidentally rewound on the VCR. Write each backward word correctly.

1. sehcirtso _____
2. sessalc _____
3. sehsurb _____
4. soedor _____
5. stnilps _____
6. sesub _____
7. sehcaoc _____
8. sehsaleye _____
9. slerrab _____
10. sehcnarb _____
11. skcart _____
12. swollip _____
13. sixat _____
14. stnerap _____
15. slrig _____
16. sehcaeb _____
17. soediv _____
18. sehctiw _____
19. selttuhs _____
20. sehctam _____

How many base words end with vowels? _____
How many base words add **s** to form the plural? _____
How many base words add **es** to form the plural?_____

Compound Countdown

Choose a word from each column to make a compound word. Write an equation from the two words as shown. Begin countdown . . . 5 – 4 – 3 - 2 - 1 - Blast off!

1. count	1 + 15 = countdown	1. storm
2. play	_____	2. room
3. my	_____	3. spread
4. brain	_____	4. body
5. home	_____	5. face
6. base	_____	6. self
7. bath	_____	7. market
8. drum	_____	8. place
9. bed	_____	9. print
10. over	_____	10. paper
11. waste	_____	11. dose
12. super	_____	12. ground
13. every	_____	13. stick
14. some	_____	14. mint
15. news	_____	15. down
16. pepper	_____	16. ball
17. bold	_____	17. times
18. fire	_____	18. basket
19. foot	_____	19. guard
20. body	_____	20. work

Use your answers from page 64 to locate these compounds.

1. Word with **ou** sound in both parts of compound

   _____

2. Begins and ends with **s** _____

3. Compounds with double consonants

   _____   _____

4. Compounds with the letters **or**

   _____   _____

5. Four-syllable compounds

   _____   _____

6. Words with **long a** sound in second syllable

   _____   _____   _____

7. Three-syllable compounds

   _____   _____   _____

   _____   _____   _____

8. Words with **oo**

   _____   _____

9. A scrambled compound: **padredbes**

   _____

10. Part of a chicken _____

11. Where recess is held _____

12. The only compound not used on this page!

   _____

Celebrate!

Use the clues and a calendar to name each holiday.
Then abbreviate the month we celebrate it.

	Holiday	Month
1. Jokes are played.		
2. Trick-or-treat		
3. Jewish winter holiday		
4. Red, white and blue		
5. He sees his shadow.		
6. Equal rights for blacks		
7. Yea, Dad!		
8. Christian spring holiday		
9. Hearts		
10. Independence for USA		
11. Abe, George, Ronald		
12. Workers honored		
13. Yea, Mom!		
14. Jewish spring holiday		
15. Birthday of Christ		
16. New year begins		
17. 1492 discovery		
18. Veterans honored		
19. Give thanks		
20. Luck of the Irish		

Word List

Presidents' Day	Veterans Day	April Fools' Day	Passover
Martin L. King Day	Father's Day	St. Patrick's Day	Easter
Valentine's Day	Hanukkah	Thanksgiving	Flag Day
New Year's Day	Halloween	Columbus Day	Labor Day
Groundhog Day	Christmas	Mother's Day	Fourth of July

Create a holiday calendar by writing each holiday under the correct month for the present year. Use page 66 to help you.

Jan.	**Feb.**	**Mar.**
_____	_____	_____
_____	_____	_____
_____	_____	_____

April	**May**	**June**
_____	_____	_____
_____	_____	_____
_____	_____	_____

July	**Aug.**	**Sept.**
_____	_____	_____
_____	_____	_____
_____	_____	_____

Oct.	**Nov.**	**Dec.**
_____	_____	_____
_____	_____	_____
_____	_____	_____

Add birthdays of friends and family on any extra lines.

Through the Year

Write the days and months in order. Put the number of syllables beside each.

JANUARY

			1	2	3	4	5
6	7	8	9	10	11	12
13	14	15	16	17	18	19
20	21	22	23	24	25	26
27	28	29	30	31		

Days

1. _____ ____
2. _____ ____
3. _____ ____
4. _____ ____
5. _____ ____
6. _____ ____
7. _____ ____

What word from the Word List is not a day or month?

_____

Months

1. _____ ____
2. _____ ____
3. _____ ____
4. _____ ____
5. _____ ____
6. _____ ____
7. _____ ____
8. _____ ____
9. _____ ____
10. _____ ____
11. _____ ____
12. _____ ____

Total number of syllables for the months. _____

What is the total for the days of the week? _____

Word List

Sunday	January	March	Wednesday
June	August	Friday	December
May	Monday	Tuesday	November
July	February	October	Thursday
April	calendar	Saturday	September

Write the day or month that comes **before** and **after** each word.

Before		**After**
_____	April	_____
_____	Thursday	_____
_____	August	_____
_____	Monday	_____
_____	January	_____
_____	December	_____
_____	Sunday	_____
_____	June	_____
_____	Friday	_____
_____	October	_____
_____	May	_____
_____	Tuesday	_____
_____	February	_____
_____	November	_____
_____	Wednesday	_____
_____	March	_____
_____	September	_____
_____	July	_____
_____	Saturday	_____

What is your favorite day? _____

What is your favorite month? _____

Review

Pages 54-55   Add each suffix correctly.

happy (ly)   _____

win   (ing) _____

share (ing) _____

day   (ly)   _____

Pages 56-57   It's minicrossword time!

education
election
vacation
mansion

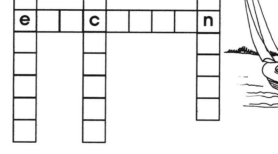

Pages 58-59   Write the contraction for each group of words.

we are   _____

will not _____

let us   _____

Pages 60-61   Make word pyramids for these words on another sheet of paper.

secretaries   **Example:** kite   k
mysteries   ki
libraries   kit
                                        kite

Pages 62-63 Write these words in the code on page 62.

videos —————————
buses —————————
girls —————————

Pages 64-65 Which word is it?
   supermarket   bodyguard   brainstorm

without vowels   **without consonants**

1. bdgrd _____   1. aio   _____
2. sprmrkt _____   2. oyua   _____
3. brnstrm_____   3. ueae   _____

Pages 66-67 Fill in the blanks with the correct word.
   Christmas   Halloween   Thanksgiving

___ a ___ ___ ___ ___ ___ ___

___ ___ a ___ ___ ___ ___ ___ ___ ___

___ ___ ___ ___ ___ ___ ___ a ___

Pages 68-69 How much is each word worth?
   A = 5¢   E = 8¢   U = 10¢   Y = 7¢
   Each consonant = 1¢
   Write the amount of each letter and then total.

Wednesday   _____ = _____
February   _____ = _____
calendar   _____ = _____